ELEMENTS OF
GROUP
COUNSELING
Back to the Basics

Third Edition

ELEMENTS OF
GROUP
COUNSELING
Back to the Basics
Third Edition

Marguerite R. Carroll
Professor Emeritus, Fairfield University

with James D. Wiggins
Professor Emeritus, University of Delaware
Adjunct Professor, Old Dominion University

Love Publishing Company
Denver • London • Sydney

Published by Love Publishing Company
Denver, Colorado 80222

Copyright © 2001 Love Publishing Company
Printed in the United States of America
ISBN 0-89108-279-4
Library of Congress Catalog Card Number 00–131241

❖ Contents

3   STARTING THE GROUP AND ESTABLISHING RULES   27

4   LEADER INTERVENTIONS   39

5 ISSUES FOR THE LEADER   55

6 WORKING WITH YOUNG PEOPLE   75

❖ Preface

Working with groups is a challenge. You find yourself in an arena with only yourself as a guide, leading a variety of groups, each with its own unique make-up requiring skilled leadership. Your colleagues may be well trained as individual counselors but unable to support you in your work because they know little about group process.

This book has the goal of helping you to facilitate member-to-member interaction in groups, in turn helping members to learn from their own experiences. We will provide some tools that you may be able to use in achieving these goals. We will address a series of questions in a number of areas, ranging from the broad base of theoretical orientation to the specifics of group formation and the logistics of facilitating a group. from the broadest philosophical orientation, you might ask the following questions:

- ❖ Should I follow any one theoretical orientation as superior to others?
- ❖ Shall I emulate a certain authority or expert?
- ❖ What do I believe, what are my values, concerning groups and myself as a leader?
- ❖ Did my training prepare me to be a successful group leader, or do I need further or more specific training?

Regardless of theoretical orientation or technical skills, more specific questions have to be addressed when actually forming and beginning a group. Some applicable questions are:

❖ Where and when should we meet? How often?
❖ How many members should the group have? Should they be screened? If so, how?
❖ What about the mix of members with regard to age, gender, intelligence level, ethnicity, and common interests? Will the group be closed or open?
❖ How long will each session last? How many sessions?
❖ Is a "blueprint" or checklist available as a guide?

As some of these questions are answered, more arise:

❖ What do I say when the members first arrive for the group?
❖ What is the best seating arrangement?
❖ What kind of instructions should I give?
❖ Do I recite a list of group rules and expectations? Should I establish goals for the group?
❖ What should I say about confidentiality, about my role as a leader, and about their role as members?

Effective leaders want to do more than merely survive. Leaders often report feeling frustrated, bored, disappointed, defeated, fatigued, and exasperated. So the questions continue:

❖ How do I encourage members to participate?
❖ What can I do if one or more members are reluctant — or worse, challenge me, or leave the group, or cry?
❖ How do I respond to difficult questions from group members?
❖ What should the rules be, and how should I enforce them?
❖ How do I achieve closure — end sessions and the series of sessions?

In regard to measuring my effectiveness, still other questions come to the fore:

❖ What can I do if I need help? Who is the best person to provide it?

❖ Can I measure my own effectiveness? If so, how?
❖ Are certain techniques, procedures, or responses more helpful than others?
❖ Would a co-leader be a good idea?

Ethical dilemmas arise as well:

❖ Should I ask a person with whom I am counseling individually to join one of my groups?
❖ If someone breaks a confidence outside the group, what steps should I take?
❖ If a group member starts to reveal too much, how should I intervene?

All of these questions, and many more, arise in the milieu of group counseling. They appear each time a group is formed, and they continue in planning, implementation, review, and evaluation of groups. With continuing experience, the solutions and answers for each group leader will change over time. We refine our skills, adapt our responses, and review our actions to see if we are really helping the group members and to determine ways we might be more effective with each new group.

The anxiety of a group leader is understandable. This book will attempt to clear up some of the confusion and conflicting information concisely and succinctly. It is intended as a take-off point in your continuing development as a group leader.

This revision incorporates, in chapter 6, a field-based research project that looks at the quantitative side of helping. It reports the outcomes of middle-school students related to here-and-now group counseling.

A new final chapter, Epilogue, is an account of how group work has affected a number of adults in personal and real ways. It is written from the perspectives of group members, as well as the leader (the senior author of this book). The group has met 3 days per year for the past 16 years, and is ongoing. A review of writing in all areas of psychology and counseling turned up no parallel to this intriguing and insightful report. The participants share snippets and snapshots of their experience, and the leader shares her insights regarding what has worked over time. This experience has been more than a scheduled annual event in the lives of 16 people. It is a here-and-now occurrence that has been, and is, an important part of their living in the present. This chapter deals not only with what has worked or helped but also with why the here-and-now group process has been successful for the participants for such a long time.

❖ Introduction to the Interactional Approach

W hat do group leaders want, and what do they need? Regardless of the group setting in which leaders find themselves, core of concerns remains relatively constant, We confirmed and amplified on that finding (Wiggins & Carroll, 1993).

For more than two decades one of the authors, Dr. Marguerite Carroll, has conducted group leadership workshops in more than 25 states and four Canadian provinces. As an integral part of each workshop, participants are asked to write their most pressing group leadership concerns. A review of the more than 21,000 questions from 4,500 participants revealed the following.

1. The work setting of participants was unrelated to the questions they asked. About 40% of the participants worked in K-12 schools, colleges, and universities. Another 48% worked in social service agencies, and the rest were from business and industry groups or private practices. A typical workshop included participants from 17 different settings and had titles of social workers, high school and elementary counselors, counselors in correctional settings, inpatient group leaders in hospitals, family counselors, and counselors or psychologists in various types of private practice.

2. The questions asked and the concerns expressed were unrelated to previous group leadership training or experiences in graduate school, workshops, books, or on-the-job

supervision. Participants with doctoral degrees who had years of experience in leading groups listed the same concerns as beginning counselors or social workers did. A recurring theme was a search for the right "recipe" for specific situations. Clearly, the participants had not embraced a "process perspective" or generalized ways of behaving that would enable them to deal comfortably with their group members' concerns.

As Yalom (1995) stated, "It is not easy to tell the beginning therapist how to recognize process; the acquisition of this perspective is one of the major tasks in the education of a therapist" (p. 151). We would add that this applies to most of the experienced group leaders who attended our workshops. Gaining a process perspective seems to be a paradoxical task. Most participants can attain it only from observing and participating in groups in which an experienced and skillful group leader demonstrates this in various specific situations. Only when these different incidents and leader actions are tied together does the participant start to grasp, then to practice, the here-and-now process perspective. Especially difficult is for an elementary counselor, for example, to understand that the same process can be applied in elementary schools and with groups of adults in transition. The terminology varies, but the process does not.

3. The types of questions asked today can be grouped in the same categories today as they were a decade ago. About 35% of the 21,000 questions workshop participants asked were related to leadership intervention and process issues. Although the other major questions asked (about 4.8 per participant) seemed to be aimed at other issues, originally, most of those questions were recognized to be linked to leadership intervention and process issues. The remaining questions could be categorized as dealing originally with organizational issues (15%), specialized techniques for a specific population (10%), establishing and enforcing group rules (6%), selecting group members (6%), uses of

group exercises (4%), ending groups (4%), evaluating leader's effectiveness (4%), leader self-disclosure and transparency (4%), co-therapy or not (3%), and goals of a group (3%). About 6% of the questions could not be categorized; they usually were linked to specific situations or settings.

Based on the questions the workshop participants asked and their evaluations of the workshops after observing and participating in a group (a feature of all workshops), we concluded that their *real* needs have not been represented. They come to workshops looking for recipes, for a "bag of tricks" from which specific leader actions can be pulled at appropriate times.

Although the need to learn more about leading groups is very real, participants usually leave with much more of a process orientation, having learned how to make relevant their group members' needs in the here-and-now. No bags of tricks or situational recipes are to be found but, rather, participants have to learn to "search in every possible direction to understand the relationship messages in any communication" (Yalom 1995, p. 153). Exercises rarely accelerate the process of therapy, so learning more activities is fruitless. *Learning the when and what of dealing with the here-and-now content brought to the group by its members is the essence of group leadership.*

Based on conducting workshops with thousands of participants, we suggest that most group leaders are unsure of themselves and underprepared to lead groups. Of course, the participants under discussion were not randomly in attendance. They came to correct their own perceived limitations in leading groups.

Group leaders not in attendance might have felt well prepared. Even so, our subjective impressions in working with counselors, social workers, and psychologists in many different settings is that this is not true for many. Yalom (1983), who has spent much of his professional life in training groups, criticized the graduate preparation of group leaders, declaring, "The ability to help members learn from observing their own process is an acquired skill that requires group training and supervision rarely available in most professional educational curriculums" (p. 20). We agree wholeheartedly with this viewpoint.

Although we are severely critical of this situation, we do not mean to blame the victims — be they counselor educators or group leaders. Courses in group counseling, group process, and group supervision are expensive curriculum areas. Class size has to be small, and skilled faculty members are not always available. Inadequate resources result in inadequate preparation for many graduate students. Inadequate preparation naturally leads to concern and problems in leading groups on the job by intelligent and well-meaning professionals, through no fault of their own.

This book in itself cannot overcome inadequate preparation or built-in problems that group leaders face on the job. Nevertheless, it may spark some awareness that prospective and current group leaders can gain the needed skill of leading in the here-and-now from a process perspective. Obtaining the needed training and supervision is not easy, and the onus is on each individual to seek out help. We also want presenters at workshops and in-service programs to take notice of the "real needs" of participants. Presenting the same inservice training to the same group year after year might be comforting to some, but it becomes wearisome to others. More is expected and needed.

Most needed, we repeat, are generic skills taught from a here-and-now perspective. The 4,500 workshop participants surveyed didn't need the games and exercises, but they did need to know how to help a group become interactional.

❖ THE CONFUSION SURROUNDING GROUP WORK

Some of the confusion and frustration regarding group work has resulted from the following.

1. *Outrageous claims.* Usually more implicit than explicit, claims have been made that group counseling or therapy

will solve all problems. These claims appeal to the "push the right button" crowd, which believes that therapy is simply a matter of finding the proper recipe. When these groups make only moderate gains, they may be perceived as failed groups, and new and different approaches are pursued frenetically. As each group fails in some manner to solve all concerns easily and quickly, the frustration rises proportionately.

2. *Questionable procedures.* A number of "experiential" articles have encouraged fringe fanatics to try anything they feel like trying, regardless of research, skills needed, or type of group. A quick perusal of counseling and psychology journals will uncover a variety of esoteric essays on group practices. For example, in a single month the contents of 20 journals revealed a variety of "how to" articles for groups, dealing with abuse-victim confrontation, assertion training for sexual minorities, children of divorce, victims of sexually transmitted disease, and adult children of alcoholics. In addition to these fairly standard articles were those dealing with "feeling colors" (group members were encouraged to describe their feelings in terms of colors), marathon sensory deprivation sessions led by paraprofessionals, massage-each-other groups, and even more extreme offerings.

3. *Emphasizing tools and techniques above communication and interaction among group members.* Almost any response, procedure, or intervention imaginable in a group setting has been supported in the printed media. The prototype is a "leader" talking to a group while thumbing through a card file to decide what to do today. This has been true especially in hospital settings, where groups meet daily or almost daily, or in schools where poorly trained counselors bring small groups together under the likeness of group counseling. This "groups-as-games approach" demonstrates little respect for the group members and probably says more about lack of leadership skills than about groups.

4. *A "one-size-fits-all," topic-oriented approach.* Some leaders assume that certain problems in living affect all potential group members in the same way and that everyone going through the same "curative" procedure will find a "cure." The topic may be children of divorce, death and dying, drug abuse, women who care too much, sexual or physical abuse — and the list goes on. Although people who agree willingly to participate in these groups might profit from a little to a lot, some schools and agencies have a mentality that all people have suffered equally, and thus, they all must go through the group.

For example, some children are relieved when parents divorce and actually do better (in school, with friends, and so on) when this happens. Others are traumatized. A child representing each extreme may be an excellent or a poor candidate for a group — and the group for each child might be one encompassing a range of concerns rather than a narrow, issue-oriented group. The guidelines for group selection should be the same as for selection to any group (these are discussed later in this book).

5. *Ignoring research findings and concurrently failing to evaluate groups.* This complaint perhaps can be leveled at practitioners most consistently. "My work is so esoteric and mystical that it can't be measured" is the defense against such charges. Compounding this problem is the uncritical acceptance by professional journals of articles that lack a research foundation while trying out "how-to" prescriptions. And professional associations urge members to conduct more group work without a concurrent plea or caution regarding the appropriateness of specific interventions. A quick review of professional group counseling journals reveals few long-terms studies. This also is the case for pre-post investigations with any type of control groups, and comparative studies with different types of interventions. The large majority of studies are "how-to" discussions with little or no acknowledgment of associated research.

In defense of the profession, Yalom (1995), more than anyone else, tells us why we do not find quantities of outcome research within the literature. He declares that "clinicians fail to heed or even believe research in which outcome is measured by before-after changes on standardized instruments, . . . for abundant clinical and research evidence indicates that change means something different to each patient" (p. 530). Nevertheless, a number of short-term designs such as those from Robison, Morran, and Hulse-Killacky (1989) are available to group workers, but backing from institutions for long-term research is lacking because of lack of funding and faculty interest. According to Yalom (1995), outcome remains the single greatest problem in group therapy research. This need has not changed in more than a decade.

If this is so, confusion regarding groups seems inevitable when we look at examples of group work. Some even seem much like individual counseling within a group setting; exchanges are primarily leader-member-leader, with other group members serving as onlookers. In other situations, the value of group work is "oversold," especially in schools. Some people need and want only group assistance. Others need and want only individual help. Some need and want both. Some want only one but need the other, or they need both types of help. We have to be cautious in what we promise and what we can deliver.

Leading groups effectively is difficult. It requires a combination of skills and learned personality/behavioral traits that mesh within the group experience. These characteristics include willingness to tolerate ambiguity, to give up power to members as they learn to empower themselves, and to use a trained ear and eye to detect meaningful verbal and nonverbal nuances in member interactions. It requires the ability to make split-second decisions in enforcing group rules, developing a "feel" for group process so the leader recognizes the emotional impact of group members' statements at any specific time, and many other skills that facilitate group growth.

Some leadership skills are learned readily and refined with practice. The willingness to use them and the attitude necessary to be a successful facilitator are part of a learned predisposition on the part of a leader-in-training. If this predisposition is present, the questions and answers in this handbook will help you learn new skills or enhance those you already possess.

❖ THE EFFECTS OF TRAINING AND THEORY

The concept of group work was popularized by the followers of Kurt Lewin in Bethel, Maine, in what became known as the National Training Laboratory. Here, people in industry and education were trained as group leaders. The emphasis was on process rather than content. Yet, decades later, Zimpfer, Waltman, Williamson, and Huhn (1985) reported, in a survey of graduate training programs, that more than 95% of counselor educators emphasized content in training group leaders. Also, they found that less than 70% of counselors-in-training actually led groups or observed groups in action. Trotzer (1989) described the training of group workers:

> It appears that we are continuing to turn out personnel who have a head knowledge of and emotional commitment to groups but who are lacking in the technical skills and experience to implement a group program on the job. (p. 192)

Still, a decade later, Trotzer (1999) affirms:

> Those weaknesses have been and continue to be addressed as a means of enhancing and solidifying the place and relevance of group work now and in the future. (p. xxiii)

The Zimpfer et al. (1985) survey also confirmed that students in the preparation program rarely are involved in practicum and supervision in group work. Graduate programs usually involve a course in group dynamics and a single course in group counseling. Thus, individuals employed in a setting that requires group work often lack the skills to do the job. An inspection of these data show that, although counselors are well aware of their needs with respect to attaining knowledge and skills, graduate programs are still operating at the basic grass roots level.

Furthermore, many people who run what are known as "support groups" have little or no formal training, although the group leaders usually have directly experienced the pain associated with the topic addressed. Although college degrees do not guarantee competent leadership, we generally suspect those who have no formal training. Many concur with Rogers (1980), who said, "There are as many *charlatans* and exploiters of people as there are uncertified" (p. 244) and, "We must face the fact that in dealing with human beings, a certificate does not give much assurance of real qualification . . . . We might also learn much from the 'uncertified' individual, who is sometimes unusually adept in the area of human relationships" (p. 246).

We agree that some people have natural skills of helping, and others think they can help and cannot. Although the consumer bears the ultimate consequence of "credentialing," all group leaders would do well to become competent, regardless of consumer demands for groups.

Training

Specific recommendations for training group leaders are available to practitioners. The Association for Specialists in Group Work (ASGW) published *Professional Standards for Group Counseling* in 1983 (revised in 1990). Although the guidelines are cited by many authors, including Capuzzi and Gross (1998), Gladding (1995), and Trotzer (1999), little evidence is available to substantiate that professional accreditation bodies enforce the ASGW standards, or that these standards are even applied in graduate training programs.

Signs of efforts to upgrade graduate training in group work appear in the work of the Council for Accreditation of Counseling and Related Educational Programs (CACREP). Included in the 1994 revision of the accreditation manual is the required supervision of students in group work for at least one fourth of the 40 hours of practicum experience. Unfortunately, the manual does not state any specified hours for graduate students to run groups or be supervised in group work during the 600 hours of required internship. Conceivably, though not likely, a graduate can leave a CACREP-accredited institution at the advanced-degree level with a bare minimum of group-work experience. Whether CACREP-accredited or not, the emphasis in most graduate programs during practicum and internship is on individual counseling. In general, group-training standards are minimal, and social workers and psychologists usually are trained outside of graduate programs accredited by CACREP. CACREP-accredited institutions are among only 133 of 450 as listed in *Counselor Preparation* [Programs, Faculty, Trends: 1996–1998,] 9th edition (Hollis, 1997).

Although the ASGW *Professional Standards for the Training of Group Workers* provide more substance, such as required content courses and hours in supervision, than the CACREP guidelines, the ASGW standards are without clout. Thus, the energy of many competent groups and individuals seems to consist of more form than substance.

Beyond the formalized training program, then, how can counselors improve their competence?

1. After having participated in a group experience during the training program, seek additional group experience as a professional.
2. Find a mentor, and seek ongoing supervision from that person.
3. Join a peer group that offers mutual support in dealing with problems that arise in group practice.
4. Attend training institutes, workshops, and inservice programs to upgrade your skills.
5. Join professional organizations that specialize in group work, such as the Association for Specialists in Group Work (ASGW) and the American Group Psychotherapy Association (AGPA).
6. Stay current with the professional literature.
7. Develop a pattern for self-reflection, examining your own motives and issues as you do group work.

8. Develop a theoretical base for your counseling that will provide you a consistent framework for group work.

Developing a Theory

The first step in exploring the uncertainties of group life is to develop a theoretical base for counseling. A pioneer, Bugental (1978) suggested that the process of selecting therapeutic goals is similar to the counselor's taking a trip into an emotional venture or journey. In preparation for that journey, Bugental spoke of the vision in the mind — a vision that describes where the traveler is going and just how the journey will unfold. In preparation, the prospective traveler listens to the accounts of others who have taken the same journey, talks to those who would lead the trip, reads descriptions of the places to visit, and finally decides whether to go. Whether to go is the personal decision of each leader and each member of every group.

Which theory, if any, does a person choose from the overwhelming number of theories available: psychoanalytic, Adlerian, psychodrama, gestalt, person-centered, behaviorism, existentialism, humanism, transactional analysis, rational-emotive therapy, and so on? The chosen theory not only will determine how the counselor will understand and assist clients but also will determine which behaviors, statements, and verbal exchanges the leader selects as important enough to emphasize in the group process.

Practitioners gravitate to a specific form of therapy depending upon personal values, training, personality, and expectations regarding the objectives and nature of counseling. Establishing a theoretical orientation is vitally important, for the theory is what provides the counselor with a road map of where, when, and how to go. It also leads to consistency in one's approach to group work. This consistency is related to how one puts groups together, develops the process plan for learning, and, finally, defines what is expected regarding the leader's therapeutic goals.

No one theoretical orientation has been shown to lead to greater success than another. Neither has any one approach to group therapy been established to be uniformly better than another (Bugental, 1978; Shapiro, 1978). Successful group work, it is generally agreed, is more a function of the leader's behavior than the leader's theoretical orientation, although theory and behavior interact in unknown ways. Studies have demonstrated that individuals of the same stated theoretical orientation do not behave in similar ways when running a group. Thus, leader behavior affects the process of group work and is as central to the process as a specific theoretical view.

Many practitioners claim they seek specialized methodological systems of group therapies that serve divergent populations, as well as specialized techniques for counselor interventions based on the assumptions that these pertain only to certain occupational groups or persons who have undergone similar experiences. Whether this is or is not true, certain aspects of group process are common to all groups, regardless of leader orientation. Basic leader management functions, many of which are addressed in this book, are common to all groups. When interventions affect the dynamics of group interaction, the goal is to induce some effect on the here-and-now process of the group.

With more than 30 years of running groups and training graduate students, we are convinced that focusing primarily on the process in the here-and-now, rather than on the content from an historical perspective of the group, is the most efficacious method. This does not deny that past events contribute to one's mode of functioning in the present, but the future-becoming-present is the main tense used in this book (Yalom, 1995).

2

❖ Setting Yourself Up For Success

P eople in groups are there for different reasons. Some need to be in a group, some want to be in a group, and some want to be in a group and should not be in a group. Our experience has helped us come to some conclusions regarding these observations. We begin with the assumption that most people who are in a group have impaired problem-solving ability and, as a consequence, react inappropriately to the environment. These individuals need help. Sometimes they seek out groups themselves, but most often individuals are "assigned," as in a hospital or agency setting. The question is: How should these groups be formed? To set yourself up for success:

❖ Exercise as much control over group composition as the overall situation will permit.

❖ If you are just beginning group work, limit your endeavor to one group, and meet within a designated period; we suggest 12-15 weeks.

❖ Shape and compose the group carefully by selecting of members properly. If possible, especially if you are a novice in leading groups, select individuals you know and with whom you have a relationship already.

❖ Select people you think will interact and have some grasp of the problems on which they should work.

❖ Do not select as members those who are chronic troublemakers, those who must dominate others, and those who have demonstrated some type of pathological behavior.

If a leader becomes frustrated with more than one group at the same time, the result, more often than not, is the loss of confidence in a potentially good leader and even flight from counseling. In other instances it has led group leaders to become dogmatic controllers of group interactions in misguided attempts to reduce friction and disagreements.

The leader should begin by making sound decisions regarding the logistics involved in running groups. This includes deciding on the meeting place, size of the group, length of the meetings, and the individuals who will compose the group. A second decision pertains to group type — open or closed, heterogeneous or homogeneous?

No specific guidelines can be set forth. Composition of a group depends upon what "feels" right rather than what "is" right (Benjamin, 1978). To this, published research provides no ready answer. Some leaders prefer to work with people who have similar conflicts; other leaders prefer a heterogeneous group composed of members with diverse populations, each with dissimilar issues to resolve. The group leader must exercise as much control over group composition as the overall situation will permit.

GROUP COMPOSITION

In forming a group, the leader has to answer the following questions: How many members should the group have? Should the group be closed or open? Should membership be heterogeneous or homogeneous in terms of the conflicts presented? Should membership be mandated or volunteered?

Group Size

A group should be large enough at the beginning so substitutions do not hinder future dynamics. A group may have as many as 12 members, but seven or eight have been found to be best for good therapeutic interaction. Smaller groups are more efficient. Large groups provide more resources from which to draw. As the number of individuals in the group increases, however, the potential number of interactions increases exponentially. For example, a group of seven has the potential for 5,040 interactions. These numbers should be convincing enough to keep the counseling group small if this is within your control.

When members drop out and new members join the group, substitutions are necessary. A policy might be established in advance as to the minimum number of sessions a member will be asked to attend before dropping out. This policy is most significant when working with a closed group.

Closed Versus Open Groups

In a closed group the membership ideally doesn't change throughout the group's life. In reality, however, members do drop out at times. If the group is small, the policy may allow dropouts to be replaced, particularly after the first meeting or two, when the group process has not solidified. To allow new members into the group beyond the first two sessions might extend the time for significant interaction drastically. This underscores the importance of screening prospective members carefully.

An advantage of the closed group is that various process stages are more clearly visible to the leader. Although the stages are not always discrete, the leader will be able to observe when the group moves from the milling-around stage (Rogers, 1970) to the more productive stages of therapeutic interaction. The closed group becomes a micro-society that develops its own history (Benjamin, 1978). Because the process tends to be more dynamic in the closed group than an open group, most group leaders prefer the closed group.

In open groups the membership changes as participants come and go. Members drop out and new members join. A disadvantage of the open group is it undermines the stability and character of the group. Norms, rules, and guidelines have to be restated constantly for the benefit of new members, and cohesiveness is difficult to establish. Rose and Edleson (1987) described new members in the open group as "strangers in a world of friends" (p. 31).

An advantage of the open group is that the counselor may draw upon a much larger client pool, allowing more people to be involved over time. And no group is truly closed. Whether groups are said to be open or closed, leaders are faced with the reality of some members' dropping out and others becoming ill or moving away.

Heterogeneous Versus Homogeneous Groups

The question of which is better, heterogeneous or homogeneous groups, cannot be answered conclusively. Discussions surrounding this topic are fervent and varied. Should a group be organized around similar conflicts or built from diverse populations with dissimilar issues to resolve?

Examples of groups formed around similar conflict areas are those dealing with divorce, single parenting, alcohol and substance abuse, weight loss, bulimia and anorexia, gay and lesbian issues, delinquency, or severe social deprivation. Often called "topic-oriented groups," these are less difficult for the leader to set up because potential members are easily identified. Participants know who will be in the group — "people like me." Knowing the topical orientation of the group before to the first meeting lessens the sense of risk for the new members. Also, conflict is reduced in topic-oriented groups because members usually have similar goals.

These homogeneous group interactions, however, may remain superficial as the issues of individual members are reduced quickly. The group focus may become tunneled as members resist broadening the discussion beyond the stated topic. With limited topical focus, the peaks and valleys of interpersonal conflict may be lacking. Thus, the limitations of topically oriented groups sometimes outweigh the benefits.

Often more challenging for the leader and group members alike is to have a mix of members with varied personalities — the rigid intellectual, the moralizer, the aggressor, the task-oriented person, the helper, the complainer. A mixed group might provide a more in-depth and powerful learning experience for those involved, as variety in personality and group conflict are more like society at large.

Our personal bias is that heterogeneous groups, which have to deal with varying degrees of vulnerability and anxiety, are the more productive groups over time. Yalom (1995) supports this view. His preference for the long-term group* is heterogeneity in make-up, with the stipulation that members should have stable ego strength.

In deciding who to include in a group, however, group leaders should beware of a "missionary spirit" that leads them to accept all who come their way. Instead, a significant goal for the professional is to define in advance how the group will be composed, with one caveat by Yalom (1995). Although he takes a strong stand in favor of heterogeneous grouping, he says, "Because of the current conditions under which group therapists work, the very topic of group composition is out of touch with the reality of everyday clinical practice" (p. 264). He says what we all know: "Virtually every contemporary group clinician in practice and the great majority in public clinics are preoccupied with problems of group integrity and survival; group composition ranks low on their list of priorities" (p. 264). Nevertheless, paying more attention to group composition would be a large step toward a more successful practice.

Mandatory Versus Volunteer Membership

Group members preferably are volunteers. The significance of individuals making deliberate decisions to be part of a group cannot be underestimated. When members are required to participate, the potential for an unsuccessful group is alarmingly high. If members participate in a group through overt or subtle coercion, it could result in attempted sabotage of group interactions. Of course, some groups are established for referred clients, by court order, for similar reasons. These groups require more intensive efforts and methods than those addressed in this beginners' guide.

---

*Long-term here implies at least 12- to 15-week sessions.

❖ DESIRABLE CHARACTERISTICS OF A GROUP

In the most effective groups, the membership is balanced, with no poor-risk members. The members accept each other, are willing to self-disclose, and are compatible. Group members have to be selected carefully to achieve these characteristics.

What potential leaders have to understand first is that selection of members and competence of the leader are directly related. A beginning leader should be cautious and not accept members whose psychological make-up requires leadership from an experienced practitioner.

Experienced group leaders learn to trust their intuition in forming a group and don't speculate too much about which member will function best with whom. Although group selection is not a hit-or-miss, it is not overly deliberate either. The experienced leader calls upon creativity, subconscious perceptions, and instinct, or the "sixth sense." Using one's intuition is much like selecting a varsity team. When observing those trying out for the team, a coach might reject a player who makes perfect shots to the basket but lacks the skills of team play. When forming a counseling group, just as in selecting a varsity team, the leader must attend to the potential interaction of all of the members.

Group Balance

Balance within the group has to do with the personal characteristics of the participating members and how those characteristics affect interaction and eventual cohesiveness. Some groups become cohesive over time. Other groups are in strife throughout most of their sessions. In still other groups, members are largely silent and relatively noninteractive. When cohesiveness is lacking, a closer look by the leader may reveal that the problem is related directly to poor group composition.

A group ideally has a dynamic balance between cognitive-reflective members who talk about their feelings (the intellectualizers) and members who express their feelings (the emoters) as well as the self-blamers (it's my fault) and the blamers of others (it's your fault). Other questions of balance include: Does the group have too many friends or work-related colleagues? Are differing viewpoints balanced so members do not feel intimidated? Without a proper mix, interpersonal dialogue lacks diversity and defenses may go up so high that the issues never will be addressed.

Gender also is to be considered in group balance. With young children, groups can be mixed. In adolescence, however, single-sex groups generally have been found to be preferable. The gains diminish in the group when girls and boys are mixed in this developmental period. At this stage, girls tend to be more serious and seek out stability in companionship. In contrast, adolescent boys are apt to have an overabundance of energy and aggression.

No Poor-Risk Combinations

Poor-risk group members include those who are withdrawn, have a need to monopolize or dominate, are hostile or aggressive, are extremely self-centered, are in extreme crisis, or are suicidal (Corey, 1995). Others who should be excluded as group members are those who are unable to conceptualize and verbalize at the level of the group, and those who are paranoid, psychopathic, and sociopathic.

Also, individuals who are drug- or alcohol-involved should not be members of heterogeneous groups. Neither should those who avoid intimacy, those who resist personal growth, and those who cannot trust or be trusted (Weiner, 1984). In addition to their adverse effects within a group, individuals with these problems stand to benefit, if at all, from individual counseling, not group counseling.

Member Acceptance of Each Other

Group members should be acceptable to each other. Warring factions and members who have personal dislikes for one another should not be in the same group. If this cannot be judged accurately in advance, the leader should prune these inappropriate members from the group after the first one or two sessions.

Willingness to Self-Disclose

Group members must be willing to self-disclose. Yalom (1995) asserted, "Group therapists may disagree about many aspects of the group therapeutic procedure, but there is great consensus about one issue; *self-disclosure is absolutely essential in the group therapeutic process*" (pp. 119-120). Self-disclosure manifests at many levels. At one level a group member must be able to share ongoing reactions to what is happening in the group. At a deeper level, members may self-disclose highly personal issues and problems—current struggles with personal issues.

The ability to risk self-disclosing (and perceived rejection) does require ego strength. A sensitive group leader will respect a group member's timing with respect to self-disclosure.

❖ GROUP COMPOSITION IN DIFFERENT SETTINGS

Group settings may be private practice agencies, or schools. Each has unique characteristics.

Private Practice

Mental health counselors in private practice often minimize screening of group members. Unfortunately, the reason for member participation — as well as motivation, possible duration of treatment, and financial resources — shapes the counselor's private practice. From the counselor's economic perspective, private practitioners may fill their groups by taking those who apply. Putting together a group in private practice is not always easy, especially when the practitioner's network is limited. Without a large referral base, the counselor may compromise the make-up of the group if there is to be any group at all. This often risks more than is imagined, as social deviates, "shoppers," and individuals with severe pathology sometimes are eager and willing to join a group.

An ongoing challenge for mental health counselors in private practice is that prospective clients often think that group work is only for "sick people," and the counselor unwittingly may set up a practice that communicates that image. Once counselors in private practice and the nature of their groups become well known, word of mouth often provides an automatic screening device.

Another issue pertains to absenteeism. Sometimes absence is manipulative behavior. Because habitual absence is destructive, the mental health counselor in private practice might wish to make clear from the onset that full fees are charged for missed sessions unless the member has a plausible reason for absence and the leader is informed in advance.

Finally, those in private practice should be wary of counseling group members both individually and in a group. Seeing a client individually and in a group simultaneously is not unethical; it just doesn't make good sense. The practice can lead to the group member's preference of sharing individually and not in the group. Some group leaders actually promote dependence of their members (Corey, Corey, and Callanan, 1993). "They may need to be needed, may depend on their work as a confirmation of their worth, or may simply need to make money" (p. 345). Corey, Corey, and Callanan go on to say that counselors must look continually at their practice "to determine whether they are fostering growth of their clients" (p. 346).

Agencies

Group members in an agency most often are referred from some outside source such as the family, school, or court. In these cases, the agency counselor may end up with a large percentage of poor-risk members because the participants are not in the group voluntarily. Lack of funds for individual help is not a positive reason for group placement, yet this is often the case. Agency counselors should be aware of the amount of resistance that these members will display and be prepared to deal with it.

On the brighter side, some agencies accept members into groups only on a voluntary basis. Participants are screened in advance, and the purpose of the group and expectations for participation are discussed.

Problems are exacerbated by referral sources who do not understand the purpose of groups or the need for screening. They often believe that involuntary placement in a group will or should achieve results that are highly unlikely. Later disappointment with the group process and the leader are sure to follow.

In contrast to private practice, many residential settings work with individuals simultaneously in group and individually. The purposes and goals of the therapeutic setting dictate this kind of practice. Group membership is acceptable under the conditions described by the agency or residential setting.

Schools

Schools generally pose the same problem for counselors that agencies do. Although school-based counselors have priorities, the institution may require that counselors take the first seven or eight people they can find or who are assigned. Schools must follow the same careful steps for screening as discussed earlier. Otherwise, leaders and their groups may become dumping grounds for problem students. Unrealistic expectations regarding groups may create the same problems that counselors face in agency settings.

School counselors must be prepared especially to make administrators and teachers aware of the purpose and role of groups in the school. We cannot "fix" students by putting them in groups. Groups are not *the* answer to behavior that teachers, parents, or administrators may see as needing remediation, especially if students are assigned involuntarily to groups. Even so, groups have a purpose in schools. The counselor has to clearly delineate that purpose and the necessity for screening members so they can benefit optimally from the group experience.

❖ Starting the Group and Establishing Rules

When a group meets for the first time, everyone is more or less anxious. To alleviate this anxiety, the leader should state the group rules during the first meeting. The instructions should be brief and to the point. Too many rules, coupled with a complex list of conditions, will only add to the emotional tension. The leader should set a strong, yet supportive tone. Group members, especially in the first meeting, respond more to tone than to what actually is said. For the first meeting, simple reminders of how often the group will meet, where, and the time may suffice.

If the group consists of adolescents or young people, the leader should recognize that young people do elbow and touch each other when they are sitting close together. Group members must understand, however, that excessive horseplay is not acceptable.

ESTABLISHING GOALS

If groups are formed at the bequest of an institution, the members have no say as to whether they want to be in a group. These groups are formed in psychiatric facilities, substance abuse centers, day treatment centers, and correctional facilities. In these settings the group leader and those in charge should discuss the institution's expectations. If the leader thinks the institutional expectations are beyond the scope of the group because of time constraints or the clinical make-up, he or she must make this known. For instance, involuntary members who are prisoners not eligible for parole have little incentive to make desirable changes.

When a group is formed voluntarily, the leader must become aware of each member's intent with respect to participation. Although group members may have specific goals for themselves when they enter the group — such as becoming more assertive in social relationships, or the contrary, becoming less aggressive and controlling with peers — goals change over time. Because goals are never static, the group leader should check out individual goals as the group progresses.

The leader's goals, whether general or process in nature, are significant. Leaders should not make their goals so specific and concrete that the group's purpose and focus become narrow. A list of general goals for the group members might be:

1. Become a better listener.
2. Develop sensitivity to and acceptance of others.
3. Increase self-awareness, and develop a sense of identity.
4. Feel a sense of belonging, and overcome feelings of isolation.
5. Learn to trust others as well as self.
6. Recognize and state areas of beliefs and values without fear of repression.
7. Transfer what is learned in the group to the outside by accepting responsibility for solving one's own problems.

The list could be much longer. Each leader should tailor and add items in keeping with his or her personal philosophy of the purpose of group work. The leader's philosophy provides direction in creating the environment for the goals to become explicit.

In addition to generalized goals are *process goals*, which — for those using the approach of this book — are related to the here-and-now. A sampling is as follows:

1. Help members stay in the here-and-now.
2. Prevent story telling related to the there-and-then.

3. Help members to confront others with care and respect.
4. Learn to give nonevaluative feedback.
5. Learn to risk by speaking from the first person.

Goals serve as general guides and should not be limiting. Competent leaders help members assess their own achievement of goals. As a result, members are able to set new goals as old ones are reached or are discarded as a result of what members learn about their interests, needs, and values within the group.

The Here-and-Now

The main concepts of this book, as well as techniques for the leader, are based on a basic approach to therapy—the here-and-now. This approach involves strategies and techniques that are easily described but difficult to carry out. By definition, the here-and-now simply means the present moment. For purposes of group work, however, the definition requires an understanding of the meaning and use of *process* as the group operates.

In group work, process unfolds through the interaction of group members. The leader must attend to not only the interaction but also to the *nature* of the interaction. The definition of here-and-now, by itself, is uncomplicated yet deceptive in operation. More often than not, leaders run groups that deal with issues, advice giving, and problem solving rather than taking advantage of events, nuances, vibrations, reactions, and unexpressed emotions within the group itself. For example, an account of a past event for which the group member is seeking advice may be of interest to the individual.

More important to the group, however, is the impact of a given dilemma on the individual members. Focusing on interaction, the leader implements strategies for connections between members using techniques (described in Chapter 4) that bring the focus of the group to the present. The here-and-now has no beginning and no ending.

Members learn about themselves from the interpersonal interaction. The key to this learning is not merely the process of experiencing the here-and-now. The leader must interpret the meaning of the process and communicate it back to the group. Yalom (1995) calls this "process commentary" (p. 129). It requires examining current behavior. "If the powerful therapeutic factor of interpersonal learning is to be set into motion, the group must recognize, examine, and understand process" (p. 136).

Process

When group members first gather and begin to engage in the process of the here-and-now, they typically begin to resist the leader. This is because the leader introduces specific interventions to change specific behaviors: "Talk directly to someone; choose a group member; don't talk to the group"; "Use the first person; say I"; "Don't story tell; stay here." These interventions seem restricting, and therefore unacceptable to group members who are new to the process. (These interventions are discussed further in Chapter 4).

Typical responses by members are anger, expressed anxiety, and sometimes even hostility toward the leader. The leader may be perceived as an irresolute ruler, never giving in to the machinations of group members who feel controlled and repressed. In reality, the leader is establishing behavioral norms, guiding the process, and assisting group members to acknowledge each other and to encourage more meaningful interaction with each other.

Initial resistance is demonstrated by the need to use the format of story telling. Reporting events that occurred outside of the group is easier than relating to group members. Acknowledging other group members' presence requires the member to recognize personal emotion, which the group member considers dangerous. Giving voice to one's feelings leaves the group member vulnerable. In the beginning stages of group process, becoming vulnerable is not a conscious decision. Through consistent, unrelenting interventions on the leader's part, though, the stage begins to be set for here-and-now responses and behaviors of group members that eventually will result in interpersonal interaction.

◆ CONFIDENTIALITY AND BREAKING CONFIDENCES

The issue of confidentiality is a prime concern to the leader and the group alike. It must be addressed from the beginning with total clarity. What is said in the group is to be confidential. Confidentiality means that group members are not to repeat to anyone outside the group what another person says. This includes describing other members' manifestations of feelings such as sadness, anger, loneliness. The leader makes a similar commitment to the group, informing members that the leader will not speak about group proceedings to outsiders. Depending on the setting, this might include parents, mates, administrators, colleagues, court officers, and so on.

Despite best efforts, no one can assure confidentiality. Adolescents are more prone to talk outside the group than adults are. To inhibit information leaks, the importance of confidentiality should be stressed at the first meeting. Group members should be advised that the leader cannot be in their presence at all times and has no direct way of knowing if members are breaking confidences. Group members, however, will likely know if anyone in the group is doing so. In those instances, members are to bring the information back to the group. After discussing the breach of confidentiality with the offending member present, other members will decide whether that member should remain in the group.

Peer pressure is more powerful than any pressure the leader imposes. The group is given the responsibility of deciding whether a member will be permitted to remain. The result is usually constructive. Rarely do group members break the trust.

The Counselor's Legal Responsibilities

Although the group must be based in confidentiality, leaders have to go beyond those bounds under specific circumstances. This is the case, for example, in reporting suspected child abuse when working with minors. Federal and state laws require reporting these suspicions to proper authorities.

Information about a minor child's plans to run away from home, or use of drugs or alcohol, may or may not be considered privileged information between counselor and client. Some states have enacted privileged information statutes. Therefore, counselors have to know the laws of the state in which they are employed. Hopkins (1989) cautioned that the determination of whether statements a minor makes to a counselor are privileged depends upon the court's interpretation: "As a general rule, communications made within a given relationship are privileged only if the benefit derived from protecting the relationship outweighs society's interest in the disclosure of the facts" (p. 15).

The Counselor's Duty to Warn and Protect

Because confidentiality is not absolute, the counselor must determine when and if it should be maintained. The group should be informed that if members discuss anything that would bring harm to themselves or to someone else, some action will be taken. Some group leaders mention specifically what is meant by "harmful content." Two issues relative to this question are illegal activities and actions that could harm self or others.

What should the leader do if group members talk about illegal activities? This question is most likely to arise when working with minors. If the illegal activities will bring harm to the group member or to someone else, the limits of confidentiality will have to be broken. The leader has stated the limits of confidentiality in the first session, so group members are well aware of those boundaries. Therefore, those who relate information of an illegal nature actually may be asking for help. Adolescents in particular often feel trapped in social situations with peers, cannot seem to extricate themselves, and have trouble asking adults for help.

A Case of Theft

Three boys in a group of seven discussed their breaking into a school building and stealing speakers off the walls in the classrooms. This violated several laws pertaining to breaking and entering and stealing public property. In discussing the offenders' behavior, the other group members warned the boys of the consequences of their behavior, which could lead to possible jail sentences, probation, and expulsion from school.

From the group counselor's perspective, the three boys clearly wanted to get the equipment back into the building unnoticed. The counselor had two choices: (a) to encourage the boys to return the equipment to the school administrator and report what they had done; or (b) to help the boys directly. Because approaching the elementary school principal involved so many unknowns, the counselor chose the latter course. The counselor took the equipment from the place the boys had stored it and returned it to the school administration, first requesting that identification of the boys who had taken the equipment not be required.

The school had notified the sheriff's office of the break-in, and the counselor was called in for questioning. The school administrator decided not to prosecute; therefore, the counselor was not required to reveal the names of the boys who had taken the equipment. The counselor told the sheriff that the boys had learned a lesson from the experience and that she would maintain a continuing dialogue with them.

This incident involved a relatively minor transgression, and the counselor felt comfortable using her own discretion about not revealing the boys' names. With more serious acts of destruction and violence, such as bodily harm to another individual, the counselor *does* have a duty to warn and protect. As laws vary from state to state, every group leader must know the state codes.

A Court Case Involving Dangerousness

An example that has been discussed extensively is *Tarasoff* v. *Board of Regents of the University of California*. Two legally prescribed duties of mental health professionals in the State of California are (a) failing to diagnose or predict dangerousness, and (b) failing to warn potential victims of violent behavior. In the *Tarasoff* case, which went to the California Supreme Court, the decision went against the psychologist and his supervisor because of failure to warn the intended victim (whom the patient eventually killed) or to warn the victim's parents.

To avoid possible litigation, professionals who work with groups or individuals must be aware of clients' rights, confidentiality, and the duty to warn and protect. A more complete examination of legal issues is available in Corey, Corey, and Callanan (1993), in which *Tarasoff* and other cases are discussed and questions are raised: "What are the responsibilities of counselors to their clients or to others when, in the professional judgment of the counselor, there is a high degree of probability that a client will seriously harm another person or destroy property?" (p. 193). These are serious professional issues that every counselor should analyze thoughtfully.

Protecting the Client: Counselor Liability

Does the counselor have a responsibility to protect clients against themselves? Of course, the answer is *yes!* Again, the counselor should have informed the group in advance that the bounds of confidentiality must be broken at times. In the case of suspected suicidal tendencies or self-destructive behavior, the counselor most certainly is obligated to act.

This may mean consulting with a professional who is qualified to make a diagnosis about a client's being potentially suicidal. Without this consultation, the counselor may be liable. Failure to have diagnosed the potential if a group member does commit suicide is grounds for a malpractice suit. Keeping a personal record of the fact that a referral has been made is especially important. This should include the time, date, place, and circumstances surrounding the reason for the referral.

Once the psychologist, social worker, or administrator has been informed (preferably in writing), the counselor no longer is liable for failure to report. Regardless of setting — private practice, school, or institution — if a client takes his or her own life, the counselor is not guilty of negligence as long as a record of adequate professional examination of the client exists (*Baker* v. *United States, 1964*).

The diagnosis must be made by a competent person, in written form, and placed securely in a file accessible to the counselor or his or her superiors. This renders school counselors less subject to lawsuits because parents, once informed of "suicidal ideation" or "suicidal behavior," have full responsibility for the child in terms of acting on their child's behavior.

What of preventing suicide itself? What is the counselor's obligation in this regard? Szasz (1986) said, "Failure to prevent suicide is now one of the leading causes for successful malpractice suits against mental health professionals and institutions" (p. 806). Does this mean the counselor must actively insist that clients seek help, should force hospitalization, or should seek other active means of preventing suicide? The answer is not yet clear.

Szasz believes that mental health professionals bear a heavy burden in respect to the moral and social dilemma posed by the act of suicide. He also warns that all mental health practitioners run the risk of being accused of professional negligence for failing to prevent the suicide of a client. This is true even though it is known that, regardless of the steps taken, many suicides cannot be prevented. If all possible steps are exhausted, the ultimate responsibility for life or death rests with the client.

4

❖ LEADER
INTERVENTIONS

Group leadership requires creating the dynamics that bring a group to an interactional state. The leader then molds this state as a sculptor molds a mass of clay, moving from an individual to sub-groups of members, to the group as a whole — combining, interchanging, compressing, or expanding an issue. The process is a three-dimensional one as the leader works to create interventions that will result in members' responding to each other. This concept of leader intervention is perhaps the most significant skill in managing a group.

Groups vary in how rapidly they learn the response patterns that foster interaction between and among group members. The leader's is responsible for fostering this skill. Therefore, the leader must be persistent in establishing the response mode for members by teaching group members how to respond to each other. The leader states and demonstrates again and again and enforces the rules until group members learn how to interact.

Once an interactional pattern is established, the leader helps shape specific types of interactions within the group. Before making an intervention with a member, the leader must have a goal in mind. A goal may be to connect two or three members, to help a member become more concrete in responding, to reflect feelings barely expressed, or to point out contrasts in member responses.

Groups have their ups and down. Leaders must be patient to avoid pushing members with inappropriate interventions. Putting thoughts effectively into words requires sensitive listening.

Understanding the meaning of what an individual is trying to convey to the group or to another member is a critical leader skill. As the leader responds, he or she is required to conceptualize the total configuration of the group itself, as well as to store possible responses to an individual that will help other group members to become involved and to interact effectively.

❖ OPENING THE GROUP SESSION

When opening the group, beginning group leaders often are uncomfortable. Sometimes the leader has the urge to mention themes from the previous meeting to give the group a place to start. This is not always wise. Although the leader's role is central in the beginning stages of the group, the leader must avoid initiating group interaction at the beginning of each session. A better way to begin is to say, in a few brief words, "Does anyone want to begin?" or, "Who would like to begin?" One of the most important criteria for inclusion in a group is motivation (Yalom, 1995). All group members are not motivated equally to start the group from session to session. Therefore, an open-ended beginning provides the proper venue for those who are prepared to begin.

❖ INTERVENTION STRATEGIES

Leader interventions are complex because of the sensitive timing and linguistic nuances required of the leader. Tone of voice, where the leader looks when making a verbal response, selecting the point to make an intervention — all have an effect on the total group. Although describing a systematic method of giving verbal cues to the group is easy (see the following pages), these descriptions don't have any magic. The leader cannot simply announce a list of do's and don't to group members ("use the first person,

"always look at someone directly when you are speaking. . .").
Instead, the "rules" should be set forth as needed. This is called
"norming the process" as the process unfolds.

Establishing Norms

Directing Comments

❖ A member starts speaking, looking directly at the leader.

Leader: "You seem to be talking directly to me. Would you
select someone in the group to talk to?"

In the early stages of a group, members want to be less personal in their interactions. Thus, members may find this direction
intimidating. More important, though, the leader is teaching the
group as a whole that members are to respond to each other and
not solely to the leader. In time, group members will recognize
that a person-to-person response is expected of them.

❖ A member gives a response but, rather than speaking to the
leader, the member's eyes wander around the group, not
focusing on anyone directly while talking in generalities.

Leader: "You're talking to the group as a whole. Can you
be more specific in what you are saying and talk to a group
member?"

From the leader's intervention, members learn that they must
personalize their responses. This does not come easily. The leader
must continue to remind group members to maintain the focus on
each other.

❖ A typical response from a group member will be, "But I
want to talk to the group."

Leader: "If you speak to a group member, you'll be making personal contact with that person, and it is important
for everyone that we personally interact with each other."

❖ While looking directly at Juan, a group member, Dave, says: "It's easy for Juan to respond because Juan has been in the group before."

Leader: "To whom are you talking?"

Dave: "I'm talking to Juan."

Leader: "Can you talk *directly* to Juan?"

Dave: "It's easy for *you*, Juan, because you've been in a group before."

In the initial statement, Dave depersonalizes the interaction by talking *about* Juan but not *to* Juan. This response is most common in the early stages. By deliberately refocusing the interaction in a gentle, yet persistent manner, the leader can help group members learn that they must talk directly to each other.

Questioning

Questioning is common in social interaction, so group members see this as acceptable within groups. Questions can be intimidating, however. Leaders should help group members "own" their questions

❖ A member, Conrad, asks a question of Ginny.

Conrad: "Do you always get nervous when you see someone fighting?"

Leader: "I'm uncomfortable with your asking Ginny a question. Instead, your question likely has something to do with you. Can you speak for yourself?"

Conrad: "Yes . . , ah . . . when I watch any kind of argument, I become so uptight I can't respond."

The leader has helped Conrad to own his feelings rather than to work them out vicariously through someone else in the group.

Members as Interpreters

❖ The leader turns an interpretation back to the responder.

In the following exchange, Yolanda has not been involved in the interaction between Elaine and another group member.

> Yolanda: "Elaine, you're really a risk taker in this group."

> Leader: "Yolanda, you've commented to Elaine that she's a risk taker. Can you talk to Elaine in reference to yourself?"

The leader has hypothesized that Yolanda really is talking about herself. Such a comment usually translates to the member's responding, ". . . and I'd like to be that way myself." The leader helps Yolanda personalize her response by verbalizing what she is experiencing. In doing so, Yolanda demonstrates some vulnerability that will lead to a deeper connection with Elaine.

> Yolanda: "I'd like to be a risk-taker like you, Elaine."

Defining Feelings

❖ A group member describes a feeling, and no one responds.

Ingrid is speaking about her fear of death. The leader senses that a number of group members identify with Ingrid, but silence prevails. If members do not receive immediate feedback after defining a feeling that is rather risky to divulge, they will risk less in the future. The leader might intervene in the following way.

> Leader: "I wonder if anyone else is feeling as Ingrid does."

> Li-Dan: "I am." (with no further explanation)

> Leader: "Li-Dan, can you respond to Ingrid and state how your feelings are similar?"

> Li-Dan: "Yes, Ingrid, I fear death myself because I never have had anyone close to me die."

> Leader: "Does anyone else relate to this?"

In the above exchange, the leader did not use the word "death" as a frame of reference. Leaders should avoid repeating word-for-word what a member has said. Instead, a synonym or a metaphor enlarges the focus. Another possible leader response is, "Does anyone feel different emotions?" An open-ended question gives all members an inroad into the group process. Rarely do all members of a group feel the same emotions or face the same issues. Linking likes and differences maximizes interaction.

A "Stuck" Group

❖ The leader wants to test the affective state of each group member because the dynamics are not thriving; the group is silent.

When the group is not moving, the following often is helpful:

Leader: "I wonder if each of you would give me an adjective describing what you are experiencing just now" (note the here-and-now focus in this statement).

Only single words are to be used, and without any explanation. Usually every group member responds. If this does not happen, the leader asks of the group, "Have we heard from everyone?" At the same time, the leader sweeps the group with eye contact to pick up those who acknowledge anyone who has not responded. Group members pick out the nonresponders quickly, usually naming anyone who has not responded. If they do not, nonverbal signals from the leader will encourage a member to address the person or persons who have not responded. The leader must not call on anyone. The norm is that *everyone* is expected to respond and the group will wait until this is done.

Examples of adjectives given in response to the leader's instruction are: perplexed, involved, fearful, excited, nervous, bored, happy, impatient, curious. If an adjective is weak, such as "okay," and the leader asks for a stronger adjective, the group member rarely is willing or able to give a deeper response. Members such as these do not feel safe in that moment in time in the group. The leader should allow members the option of playing it safe until they are ready to go deeper.

Teaching the group that getting in touch with emotions is important. The next step is to link like words and ask the members to discuss with each other the personal meaning of the adjectives given (e.g., perplexed, impatient, bored.) Most adjectives can be linked with another of similar nature. In linking like words, the group becomes more interactive, and nondisclosers find a safer way to respond. Nondisclosers in particular are connected with others and are able to interact at a more meaningful level.

Lack of Feedback from Another Member

❖ A group member talks to another member, who does not respond.

The leader should recognize this omission — especially Anita's, who does not respond.

> Leader: "Marge, you're talking to Anita, so you have some felt connection. I sense that you want to hear from Anita?"

> Marge: "Yes, I'd like to hear from Anita."

> Leader: "Can you give your reason for your connection and speak directly to Anita?"

Sometimes, asking for the reason for the desired connection (in this case, Anita back to Marge) provides the group (and the leader) with more content to work on. In the following response, Marge supplies a reason.

> Marge: "Anita, I've liked things you've said earlier because you say things so clearly."

Although the form of praise in this response is not profound, it could instill a deeper connection between Anita and Marge. The leader should watch for a later time when another member makes the same statement to Anita. At that time, the leader can link the three, referring to both present and past events.

A second example of the above is:

> Leader: "Yvonne, I notice that you selected LaShonda. Is there a special chemistry?"

> Yvonne: "Yes, I feel that LaShonda feels as I do, from what I heard her say earlier in the group."

Notice how Yvonne is depersonalizing the response to LaShonda, yet what is being said is important. To help the interaction further, the leader says:

> Leader: "Yvonne, can you be specific and state that feeling? Also, can you speak directly to LaShonda?"

This example is similar to the prior one, yet the leader uses different words ("chemistry"). Group members usually understand what "chemistry" means.

From the response, "what I heard her say earlier in the group," the leader should ask Yvonne to be concrete about what she means. In addition, the leader must remember the content of LaShonda's earlier response. Yvonne may be guessing what LaShonda felt, so the leader should watch for accuracy. If a member labels, the leader will want to follow up immediately.

Labeling

When a group member makes a diagnosis about another member's behavior, such as, "You're disgusting," this is labeling. The counselor can change the psychological effect on the group member being labeled (as well as the group as a whole) by responding with the statement that follows Seong's interpretation:

> Seong: "Mike, you're really hostile."

> Leader: "Seong, I'm uncomfortable with your describing Mike. Only Mike can tell us what his responses mean. I don't know what Mike's responses mean either. *He* has to tell me and the group."

The leader is helping the member to understand (and teaching the group as well) that only Mike, and no one else, can describe his own feelings. The group learns that each person must speak for himself or herself.

The leader does not encourage, or even allow, Mike to respond to Seong's comment. In this instance, group members are learning that they, too, will not be labeled and that the group is a safe place to be.

In addition to relieving the psychological effect, the leader is informing all group members of a new behavioral norm: No labeling allowed! Norms are an ongoing part of the teaching process. Not only does the leader teach the group the norms of "do's and don'ts," but also models similar behavior.

Leaders, too, have been guilty of labeling: "You're a passive-aggressive type"; "You have an addictive personality." At no time is the leader to label or diagnose the behavior of a group member.

Encountering Silence

One of the major fears of group leaders is to encounter silence from members. If this happens, what can the leader do? What does the leader say? Does the leader just let the silence go on and on, and thereby put pressure on the group?

In the first place, the leader must determine whether the silence is active or passive. This is easy. An aura like a soft breeze permeates the group when the silence is active. If this is not the case, the leader has one of three choices: (a) focus on the group as a whole, (b) respond to one group member, or (c) remain silent. Because members are not in the group merely to be silent, the last recourse is least desirable. The second choice may take those who have not responded "off the hook" and the group may lose ownership for the silence. Therefore, the wisest choice is the first, a response to the group as a whole. The following is an example:

"What's difficult right now?"

Inevitably someone in the group will respond. Typical responses are, "saying something meaningful," "the silence," or "being the first to talk."

Any number of responses are possible. With each response, the leader will have the opportunity to expand on the words in an attempt to connect one member with another.

A second example is:

> "Where are each of you connecting? With whom? Would you name that person or persons?"

This lead is useful when the group is bogged down and the leader wants to check where members are in relation to each other. Once members all have made a connection by giving the name or names of fellow group members, the leader decides how to assist them in verbalizing the reason for the connections. Rarely do members fail to make a connection with another group member. Those who are left out may become involved by discussing their reaction to not connecting to others in the group. This lead should not be used in early sessions when the group members are too tentative and lacking in trust to name others with whom they sense a connection.

The examples given are not gimmicks to be used each time the leader finds an individual member, or the group as a whole, at a standstill. Groups catch on quickly to leader ploys. They will resist and wait for the leader to modify the process or introduce new topics — neither of which leads to personal responsibility for group membership.

Additional Counseling Leads

Sensitive timing and tone of voice are fundamental to productive interaction when using the following leads. Some can be used early in the process, and others well into the process. Leaders should respond in few words and simple language.

Bringing the Content to the Here-and-Now

❖ I know this has real meaning for you, but how does it relate to *here*?

❖ I got the sense that you left with some feelings last session. Where are they now?

❖ Something reminds you of the outside. Can you bring it here?

❖ Stay here. You moved away — went out there.

❖ I sense a hidden agenda — messages I'm missing. I'm not sure what's happening here.

❖ Where are you right now? You're talking about the past. Talk about what you're feeling (or "experiencing") right now.

Assisting Members to Look Inward

❖ I think you're saying you want to be liked. Do I have that right?

❖ You want Peter to be somebody different?

❖ I get the sense that some of you are a little impatient. Anyone want to respond to that?

❖ I sense that you're really feeling something. Can you catch hold of it?

❖ You're saying that it's hard to be real because something gets in the way. Can you talk about what gets in the way?

❖ You're telling Yvonne what you want for her. What do you want for yourself?

❖ I see people responding to you nonverbally, but I'm not hearing from you. What do you experience when you get those signals?

Linking: Joining Individuals Together

❖ Let me help you. You're saying you feel Jo Ann didn't hear you? Is anyone else in the same place?

❖ I wonder if anyone else is where Ben is?

❖ Who are you talking to? Can you respond directly to someone?

❖ I'm wondering if you see part of yourself in Rona from what she has just expressed. Would you feel comfortable talking to Rona?

❖ Would you like to say anything else to each other?

❖ What do you want to say to Mary Anne?

❖ Some people right here may share some of your feelings. Would you like to hear from any of them? Would you like to say whom?

❖ I wonder if anyone in the group can identify with what Tasha is saying?

❖ I don't know where the rest of you are. Can anyone respond to Joshua?

❖ I'm wondering if anyone shares Shantelle's feelings?

❖ I wonder if anyone else can help us understand what Drew is trying to say about his experience?

❖ I'm not sure what meaning that has for you. Can you tell someone?

❖ You're talking to the group. Can you be specific and talk to someone in the group?

Personalizing Group Members' Experience

❖ Can you speak for yourself?

❖ Can you try to rephrase that and talk about yourself?

❖ Different things are important to different people. What is important to you now?

❖ What are you saying about yourself?

❖ I'm not sure what meaning that has for you.

❖ You're uncomfortable because. . . . Could you help us to get to where you are?

❖ I'm not sure where you are.

❖ You're in a different place. Can you help us get to where you are?

❖ What does it mean to you... that no one connected with you?

Responding to the Leader's Authority

❖ I'm glad you could tell me that (if a negative feeling is expressed to the leader about the leader).

❖ You're speaking to me. Can you respond to someone in the group?

❖ By always responding to me, you're saying I'm important. I'd like the group members to be more important to you than I am. I'm really not as important as they are.

❖ You don't like the way I lead the group. I'm glad you can tell me that (with no more explanation from the leader).

Ending a Group Session

❖ We have about 10 minutes left (with no more explanation)

❖ Can we leave it here right now?

❖ Are we all comfortable leaving it like this?

❖ I'm going to stop. It's time. (having warned the group earlier that 15 minutes remained).

❖ What will you take away from here? (at end of the final session)

❖ You're having trouble saying goodbye. (end of final session)

❖ ISSUES FOR THE LEADER

some specific issues that arise in groups include problems with structured exercises, how much the leader should self-disclose, the leader's negative feelings toward some members, persistent nondisclosers, latecomers and absentee members, silent members, scapegoating conflicts, monopolists, concurrent individual and group counseling, extending a group's life, group conflict, and challenges to the leader's authority. These concerns are the topic of this chapter.

STRUCTURED EXERCISES

A leader can easily misuse structured exercises in an attempt to draw group members into a dynamic interaction. Instead of doing the hard mind work of conceptualizing the here-and-now inexperienced leaders may grasp for a technique without focusing on the process.

Leaders commonly use structured exercises in the early stages of the group in an attempt to bypass the frustration of getting started. In later stages of the group, a leader may use exercises to accelerate the pace of the group. More often than not, the pace is accelerated, but in doing so, the leader gambles. Yalom (1995) described the consequences of hastening the process: "The group pays a price for its speed; it circumvents many group developmental tasks and does not develop a sense of autonomy and potency" (p. 445). The group loses its sense of autonomy because the exercise becomes the focus of the group. In addition, a new process norm is introduced, prescribing that the leader will do the work of the group when the process bogs down.

Further, structured exercises reinforce dependency on the leader by placing the focus on the leader, as well as putting the leader in the position of becoming the prime helper. As a result, group members become less inclined to help each other. Dependency on structured exercises may cause group members to "deskill themselves" and "divest themselves of responsibility" (Yalom, 1995, p. 447).

Sometimes, rather than accelerating the pace, the affective elements of the group slip by and the group reaches a deadend. When a deadend is the result of a condition the leader created (an exercise), the leader is forced to assume responsibility for the group and deal with the consequences of the exercise.

Finally, members may be pressured or even feel coerced to respond to an activity. Shapiro (1978) strongly advocated timeliness, appropriateness, and member consent as basic conditions when using structured techniques. In the long run, the group process without using structured exercises provides a learning climate that is more productive. Members are better able to assume their own agendas than when the leader sets the theme.

❖ LEADER SELF-DISCLOSURE

Beginning group leaders often ask, "How much should I reveal to the group to give members a sense of me as a person?" As facilitator of the group process, the leader's responsibility is to the participants. Beginning leaders (and even those with a wealth of experience) often have a strong need to be accepted and approved by group members. The novice leader may nurture this desire for approval by sharing personal events. When the leader makes the mistake of sharing intimate details in response to a comment from a member such as, "You've heard a lot from us, but we don't know anything about you," the leader may become trapped into answering other demands of group members later in the process. For example, the leader may want to inform the group at the beginning that he or she was once a substance abuser but revealing the intimate details of the abuse is not productive to the process.

To remain distant, to orchestrate the process yet be present psychologically, and to communicate with empathy to a given member in moments of joy or pain is an art. The leader's task is to achieve the proper balance of the self as a whole person effectively and cognitively, yet remain responsible for responding to the intricate dynamics of the group. To help members, the leader has to become *involved* emotionally but must not become *entangled* emotionally in the problems of group members or in self-seeking approval from them.

Inappropriate self-disclosure

> Member: "I really don't feel comfortable talking about myself"

> Leader: "That really provokes me. You've got to assume more responsibility in this group."

A more appropriate response

> Leader: "I know you want to hear from me, but how your fellow group members respond to your statement will have more meaning to you because they are more important to you than I am. Would you address someone in the group?"

Benign Questions

Some questions are so harmless that, when the leader answers them, they have no long-term effect on the group. Not all group members want this information, but when the leader avoids answering, thinking the information is irrelevant, some members might cease to self-disclose and thereby interrupt the group process. In his years of experience as a group leader, Friedman (1989) found that answering benign questions without elaboration did not lead to disruption of the group process. Some examples of benign questions are:

> Members: "Are you married?" "How long have you been doing this?" "Do you have children?" "Do you have a Ph.D?" "Are you a doctor?"

When the Leader Has Specific Feelings About a Member's Behavior

The following is an example of here-and-now self-disclosure. Other group members learn that the leader will look out for their welfare in the group as well.

> Leader: "I'm uncomfortable in how you're talking to Jonas. I'm uncomfortable with your constant questioning of Seong. Can you speak for yourself?"

❖ LEADER'S NEGATIVE FEELINGS TOWARD A GROUP MEMBER

The leader will care for some group members and will find others irritating. The irritant even might be a person in the group to whom the group as a whole responds favorably. If this is so, the problem of leader irritability usually is related more to the leader than to the person within the group.

When negative feelings arise, sensitive leaders will be wary of placing their own agenda on that individual by responding inappropriately. Instead they should view this as an opportunity to model helping and helpful behaviors to group members. How the leader resolves personality difficulties with a group member varies. Self-examination, introspection, and consultation with a fellow professional are avenues to consider.

The leader must ask, "What's going on with me and this person?" Once the issue is resolved from a sound clinical perspective, the leader's negative reaction may be dispelled. Too often, leaders expect themselves to be perfect, as do their supervisors, colleagues, and clients. To not like a group member is legitimate, but the safety of group members is primary, and dealing with negative reactions is crucial to the group process.

❖ PERSISTENT NONDISCLOSERS

Verbally active group members do not always self-disclose in meaningful ways. Statements to other group members such as, "I'm so glad you expressed yourself;" "I'm happy you can tell us how you feel," or, "I'm glad you could talk to Peter that way" actually impair the group process.

A better response would be, "I'm so glad you expressed yourself, because I want you to be a member of the group and I need to hear from you. What you say helps me to be in touch with myself." The difference in this response is that it includes a disclosure about the self in relation to the group member.

In the early stages of group life, members rarely confront nondisclosers because use of the first person is deceptive. Some time will pass before group members realize these responses have little substance. Those who do not self-disclose, or who respond to others on an intellectual plane, have spent a longtime blocking affect from their experience.

Yalom (1995) suggested that when a member does not self-disclose, the person may perceive self-disclosure as dangerous — dangerous because it makes one vulnerable to control by others. Ohlsen, Horne, and Lawe (1988) advised that these individuals may be emotionally debilitated. Once the dike of emotional suppression is released, the member might fear being lost in a release of emotion in which total control is forfeited and the emotions prevail. Yet, self-disclosure is the lifeline of the group. Without it there is little risk-taking or subsequent progress. Thus, the leader must not be intimidated by the resistance but instead should be encouraged to search out answers to the following questions:

1. What feelings does [this person] have in common with other clients?
2. How may I respond to these common feelings and facilitate affiliative feelings among them?

3. How may I prepare [this member] to request and use feedback from fellow clients? (Ohlsen, Horne, & Lawe, 1988, p.
194)

❖ LATECOMERS AND ABSENTEES

Latecomers and absentees constitute a common problem for
group leaders. Absentees usually are displaying a form of resistance. Habitual absentees attend a few sessions, then miss one,
come to the next, and then miss again. If the first absence is early
in the group sessions, it might denote a lack of commitment to the
group. One way of avoiding the therapeutic impact of a group is
simply not to show up (Trotzer, 1999). Although they may be
physically absent from the group, absent members are not for-
gotten. For the group members present, there is no such thing as
"out of sight, out of mind" (Trotzer, 1999).

The leader's first priority is to maintain the integrity of the
group. Sometimes the needs of individual members must be
placed second to this end. An example of addressing group needs
rather than individual needs is when a person perceived by the
group as a problem member is absent. During the absence several
group members refer to the problem member, declaring that they
are glad the person is not there. The leader must not let the comments slide or even suggest that when members are absent, they
are not to be discussed. Instead, the leader should help group
members deal constructively with their feelings about the absent
member. This is an area of conflict for many group leaders as
they get caught up in the ethics of the dilemma.

When a member is removed, other group members often
become defensive. Although they may be hostile or angry at first
(members see the possibility of the same thing happening to
them), some group members voice approval of the leader's
action. When opinions differ, group members will have an opportunity for a productive here-and-now dialogue. Because of the
effect on the group process, the leader should remain firm after
making the decision to remove a member. Groups are democratic

only in providing security to individuals; the leader is the only voting member.

Finally, the leader might recommend to the chronic absentee that individual counseling may be a more reasonable alternative in seeking help. This is not meant to be pejorative. The intent is still to work with the client, but alone.

Like absenteeism, lateness is disruptive. Chronic latecomers show resistive behavior from the start. Their excuses often sound most convincing.

"The babysitter was late."
"I had to see a student unexpectedly after school."
"The traffic was terrible."
"I had an important business appointment."
"My car wouldn't start."

Do you risk losing the member by holding the line? Do you start the group time later than specified? Do you let the person come in late and ignore it? Answers to the above relate to the group norms established in the beginning. In our experience, the most productive way to curb lateness is to start! Group members entering late are given no response to their reason for being late; the group already has begun.

Some leaders try to negotiate with the latecomer. Friedman (1989) spoke of the dangers of negotiating an agreement to tolerate a member's tardiness. He used the example of buying time, as British prime minister Neville Chamberlain requested in Munich in 1938: "Chamberlain. . . agreed to Hitler's occupation of northern Czechoslovakia in exchange for a promise of 'peace in our time.' World War II began the following year" (pp. 39-40).

Finally, to curb habitual lateness, the leader might have to resort to dropping the member from the group. The most productive way of dealing with lateness, however, is within the group context and not on a one-to-one basis. The content becomes good fodder for group process. The leader first should try to instill behavior change, then deal with the cause of the absence. The cause most often is related directly to the group itself.

Chronic absentees and latecomers need help. Because these members can damage the group process, the counselor has to make important decisions regarding them and the group.

❖ SILENT MEMBERS

The problem of dealing with silent members in a group has no easy solution. Silent members are those who respond rarely and, when they do, their response is so brief that it provides little to which anyone can react. Silent members come in many forms. A group member might feel unworthy of participation. Or the person's social milieu or cultural background might render verbalizations in that uncommon setting. Observing and taking it in is the behavioral norm for some people. Others use silence as a form of manipulation. Still others appear resistant because they are naturally shy, inhibited, embarrassed, fearful, or hesitant. Some silent members communicate behaviorally rather than verbally; they cannot assign words to their subjective experiences. In any case, leaders commonly observe a group member blocking out all present experience, remaining devoid of affect, and responding to most interactions with a blank stare.

For example, the leader asks a member, "How are you feeling right now?" The answer is, "Fine." Yet, the member's face is flushed, the neck is red, and the lips pursed. To engage the silent member with the group, the leader may point out or ask if other group members have observed the difference between what the member's emotions show and the words say.

Another approach is to ask, "Have we heard from everyone?" Aware of the silent member, group members likely will point out who has not responded. This may be sufficient to draw out a silent member.

No one best approach works in getting a response from a group member who persistently chooses to remain silent. If the leader asks directly to hear from the silent member, the response is likely to be "safe" and most always related to the there-and-then.

For example, "I was remembering when I was in another group . . ." or, "I'm just listening to each person." At this point an inexperienced leader is apt to inform the member that he or she has to participate or the leader may reiterate the group contract (if there is one) that all members have agreed to participate actively. The danger here is that when the leader prods, the member may gain control of the process. In addition, whenever a leader initiates an intervention directed at a member who is withholding participation, the possibility always exists that the member is withholding to manipulate or to punish the leader. On the other hand, the member may be so conflicted by the probing that a response is unattainable.

A rule of thumb is to refrain from initiating a direct response to the silent member. Instead, the leader might observe how the group responds to the silent member and use strategies that require the group members rather than the leader to deal with the individual member. In most situations the leader must observe to see if the silent member has withdrawn psychologically or is really involved. All of the above require different approaches from the leader, depending upon the dynamics of the silence.

SCAPEGOATING

Scapegoating is one of the most common and most frustrating problems for group leaders. Most often the person scapegoated is the object of displaced aggression. The initial challenge for the leader is to recognize scapegoating in the first place, then to act on it quickly, attempting to find the source of the aggression. Scapegoats have their own unique style. They may sermonize, be contentious, act dumb (not "getting" what everyone else understands), patter endlessly, ruminate about past events, or remain untouched by any appearance of intimacy. Some leaders attempt to encourage group members to give feedback to the scapegoat. When sharing their perceptions of the scapegoat's behavior, members may unload their aggression and vent their negative feelings on the scapegoat. When this happens, group cohesiveness may shift to group hostility, taking various and subtle forms. The latter is more evident in adult groups than in groups composed of young children and adolescents.

Because so much aggression is directed toward the scapegoat, an inexperienced leader might seek to protect the scapegoat against group attack or, even worse, focus group interaction on the person being scapegoated. Concentrating on the scapegoat will be fruitless. Instead, the leader should search out the cause of the group anger, whether it is toward the leader (which is often the case) or from some other source. The latter may become impossible to determine when scapegoating has gone on for several group sessions. This is good reason for leaders to act quickly at the first sign of scapegoating.

As a safeguard, leaders also should look at their own feelings when analyzing the problem before them. If the urge is to protect the member who is a scapegoat, what began as a problem between the group and the scapegoat might become a problem between the leader and the scapegoat versus the group. In this case, the group no longer has a leader. On the other hand, if the scapegoat is an irritant to the group and the leader, the dynamic becomes one of the leader and group versus the scapegoat.

Sometimes group members attack a scapegoat because the attacking members see traits in the scapegoat that they do not like in themselves. Shulman (1979) provided the example of youngsters who are having trouble in school, describing how peers pounce on every defect they can find in a group member who is having difficulty in school and experiencing the same problems as the peers — perhaps more severely, yet identical. The leader is urged to avoid siding with either the scapegoat or the group. Each must be helped to recognize the meaning of his or her behavior.

Kottler (1994a) presented another point of view on the scapegoat.

> He or she "marches to the beat of a different drummer," which can either be tremendously distracting or wonderfully enriching in terms of adding diversity to interactions . . . . In the worst case, the scapegoat . . . becomes a destructive distraction,

unwilling or unable to abide by even the most basic group
norms and rules. He or she is more than one step behind the rest
— a whole flight of stairs behind and likely never to get any
closer. (p. 163)

In sum, cohesive groups are able to freely express negative
feelings toward themselves and the leader. When scapegoating
occurs, group cohesiveness is endangered, possibly destroyed.
Thus, scapegoating can be hazardous if it is unchallenged.

GROUPS IN CONFLICT

When group norms have been established and the group has a
sense of cohesiveness, conflict can be a source of healthy interaction in the group. When conflict is out of control, or occurring
too early in the group process, however, members may become
disagreeable, antagonistic, and even hostile. The leader must not
become intimidated by group strife. When conflict does occur,
the leader must be vigorous in handling the interaction while art-
fully attempting to figure out the cause of what happened and
why. This not only demands an instant diagnosis in studying the
group members but also requires an examination of the leader's
own contribution to the problem.

Kottler (1994a) offered possible reasons for the latter, such as
the ". . . leader's need for approval, feelings of inadequacy, unre-
solved personal issues, inconsistent enforcement of rules, or
human error" (p. 168). From the onset of conflict, then, the group
leader must be sensitive to the group process and be aware of his
or her own sensitivity to the group's expression of anger.

Expressions of anger can take the form of discord, friction,
argument, and disharmony. Although Yalom (1995) stated the
prime prerequisite for successfully managing anger is cohesiveness within the group. "Management" and complete "abrogation"
of anger obviously differ. The goal is not to eliminate conflict
but, instead, to use it for therapeutic activity. The leader will want
to clarify communication and assist group members to "deal

directly with one another no matter how angry they become" (p. 348–349).

Spinal's (1984) interventions, cited in Kottler (1994a, p. 169), suggest possible interventions in handling resistance.

Intervention	*Example*
Validating resistance:	"It's helpful sometimes for us to move slowly."
Confronting resistance:	"You keep taking the focus off you."
Setting limits:	"You keep complaining about what others are doing to you."
Didactic intervention:	"This is a normal and predictable stage."
Directing the process:	"What is your reaction to that?"
Clarifying the process:	"Things seem different with only two of you contributing."

❖ MONOPOLISTS

The question that mental health professionals in our study asked most frequently was "How does the leader handle the monopolist? (Wiggins & Carroll, 1993). More group leaders have suffered anguish when the person's endless chatter, interruptions, irrelevant stories, interrogations, filibustering, or identification with every group member's problems begins to control the group.

Individuals monopolize for numbers of reasons. The monopolist may feel a certain sense of power and use this power to avoid intimacy by keeping others at a distance. Also, ongoing compulsive intonations are seen as a way to reduce anxiety. Or "they may feel a sense of entitlement, that they are more important than others in the group" (Kottler, 1994a, p. 177; 1994b).

The monopolist's effect on the group is almost always detrimental unless the leader actively intervenes. If the group responds to the monopolist, the response usually is hostile, such as "shut up," "we've heard enough from you." Thus, the leader must intervene by interrupting, as group members will not be able to interact with the monopolizer; they are not comfortable or sophisticated enough to handle confrontation, especially when the group is new or inexperienced. The interruption should not be in the form of an attack, although the monopolizer might see any response from the leader as a criticism.

Ordinarily, groups can handle their own problems but in the case of the monopolist, that person has gained control of the group. The monopolist needs to hear about the repercussions of his or her behavior on the other group members. In most instances the group leader recognizes that other group members are frustrated, irritated, or bored with the monopolizer. Thus, a leader statement such as the following is suggested in response to Jane, a monopolizer: "I sense, Jim that you're frustrated with what Jane is saying. Can you tell Jane how you're frustrated?"

In addition, to help monopolizers become more aware of their presence in the here-and-now, as well as to look at the consequences of their behavior, a group leader might ask, "What do you want from the group now that you've said all this?" "How do you perceive the group members responding to you?" Another technique is to set time limits: "You have a lot to say, but you have only two more minutes." Or suggest, "The next time can you contribute to the group in ten words or less?"

Monopolists should not be silenced. Instead, they should be helped to be heard differently — heard without the smokescreen that prevents others from "knowing" the person. Because group members are sensitive to leader interventions, silencing a monopolizer may desensitize other group members with the thought that "this could happen to me."

Finally, monopolizers are not always ready to learn quickly. Because the monopolizer can terrorize or frustrate group members to the point of incapacitating the group, the leader must govern responses to the group members so they feel all will be treated equally. The leader also can be guilty of reinforcing the monopolizer's low self-esteem and feelings of worthlessness by constant tutoring. Therefore, "Good timing is necessary; there is no point in attempting to do this work . . . in the midst of a firestorm. Repeated, gentle, properly timed interventions are required" (Yalom, 1995, p. 375).

◆◆ CONCURRENT INDIVIDUAL AND GROUP COUNSELING

A group member may be receiving individual counseling also. Do persons who participate in individual and group counseling simultaneously gain equal benefits? Leaders have many views on this issue. A complication in concurrent counseling arises when a member uses individual counseling to "drain off" from the group. A group member sometimes seeks out the leader for private discussion of a problem. The leader must assist the group member in bringing the problem back to the group. This prevents "drain-off" from the group.

Concurrent individual counseling and group counseling often is found in a school setting when a student is in a school-based group and at the same time is involved in individual counseling with an outside counselor. In these cases the school counselor could contact the outside counselor (with the permission of the student or parent) and share professional concerns with that counselor. Concurrent individual and group counseling also is found in some psychiatric settings in which constant intervention with patients is vital to treatment. Generally, though, concurrent group and individual counseling should be avoided. Certainly, the same counselor should not do both.

◆◆ EXTENDING THE TIME LIMITS

Termination may refer to ending a single session or to the group in its final session. Neophyte leaders must learn how to manage group time from the beginning. Extending the time of a single session is not a good idea. Group work is a learning situation, and group members must learn to adhere to guidelines and deal with material in a predetermined time frame.

A member's bringing up material at the last minute is often a form of manipulation. Extending the time would give undue power to the group. The group then would seek additional ways to manipulate the leader. Most issues can wait until the next session. If a group member expresses some urgent issues during the final session, the leader should close the group as planned and tell the member that he or she will be seen after the session is over. This way, the entire group is informed that whatever has been left undone will be handled.

The process of working up to the final session is important. Assuming that the group is meeting for a predetermined number of weeks (which is good practice), the group should be prepared for termination when the last few sessions approach. The leader should remind the group that "we have three more sessions," and so on. If the group is reminded too soon that closure is near, however, some groups will not bring up new material or will attempt to close early. Good group time is lost by closing too soon.

❖ CHALLENGING THE LEADER'S AUTHORITY

In working with a group, one of the leader's goals is to provide maximum opportunity for individuals to expose their behavior, give and receive feedback, experiment with new behavior, and develop lasting awareness and acceptance of self and others. The verbal content of the group — the "curriculum," so to speak — is what each member brings to the group in an emotional and interpersonal context.

At the beginning, group members typically view the leader as a source of expectation, authority, and gratification. Much of this expectation is a result of the socialization process, wherein members have been culturally imbued with respect for and dependence upon authority. In the eyes of the members, the leader is the source of authority in the group. This poses a problem for the leader, as the group will not move forward until the members resolve their basic dependency needs toward authority (in this case, the leader). Initially, group members typically expect the counselor to lead them, to present topics for discussion, and even to start each session.

Members' reaction toward authority is also symbolic. The leader represents a significant ideology toward authority, which varies from member to member. Typical symbolic references toward authority are the church, parents, teachers, the boss, government, the police, and so on. As a result, during the group process, members will act out dependency needs resulting from a lifetime of internalized responses toward authority. Individuals respond to authority in subtle and different ways, often through comments that suggest the leader is doing things to have power over the group.

When a member is uncertain about his or her place in relation to the leader, emotions are conflicting. The member wishes to be "taken care of" by the leader on the one hand, yet distrusts the leader on the other. This replicates how members respond to the various symbols of authority in life. As a result, each member will demonstrate his or her dependency needs toward authority in a negative or hostile form. Acting-out behavior in this case can be either overt or disguised. Regardless, the message to the counselor is: "Can you handle what I'm really like?" "Where is my place with you?" "Where do I fit in?" The leader's goal, therefore, is to unfreeze dependency needs of group members by interventions that support independence on the part of members.

As the group process evolves, the leader looks for certain cues from group members that are directed toward the leader in a negative or challenging form. Examples of challenging the leader are:

"Every time you respond to me, you're telling me what to do, where to look."

"As the leader, you block the group by changing the focus."

"You said the group isn't a group yet. I don't like what you said, because I felt we were becoming a group."

Responses such as these may not accurately replicate what the leader actually has said. When a group member is challenging the leader, the challenge is what is important, not the accuracy or inaccuracy of the challenge.

When responding, the leader will want to support the group member for displaying openness toward the leader. A supportive response informs the member that the leader has made no conscious attempt to be hostile or controlling. Also, an intervention that "confirms" any one member promotes growth and autonomy within the group and unfreezes the dependency needs of other members toward the leader.

One word of caution to the leader here is that all group members do not have the same dependency needs. Some resolve their issues with the leader early in the group, in subtle and less obvious ways. The leader would be making a mistake to push all members to deeper clinical levels about their basic dependency on authority. This could anger members who have resolved their dependency needs toward authority.

A typical response by the leader to a group member who is challenging the counselor's authority might be: "I'm glad you could tell me that. I'm glad you could tell me how you feel about what I do." The leader is saying to the member, and subtly to everyone else: "Yes, I see your imperfections, and I still care about you. I can handle whatever you bring this way."

Confrontations toward the leader's authority may occur in the first session or after a number of sessions have passed. Regardless of when the confrontation occurs, the leader must respond to each person whenever the challenge arises. The leader should not assume that all members experience group interactions in the same form or manner. Some have to receive the reassurance individually from the leader as they are unable to internalize the subtlety of what the leader said to a member previously.

The objective, therefore, is to develop an effective membership role for each person in the group. Responses to authority are a hidden dimension in the process. The leader is the resource to help members increase their authenticity by becoming less dependent, submissive, and conforming.

6

❖ WORKING WITH YOUNG PEOPLE

Leading a group of young people involves strategies related to organization that are different from strategies implemented for adults. The tumultuous world of the adolescent, in particular, is fraught with experiences unlike those of adults and creates an enigmatic haze around their attitudes and behavior. Adolescents are constantly changing: in body image, in mood, in emotions as a result of hormonal development, in thinking and patterns of response to events in their lives. As a result of these changes, adolescents in groups are apt to be more cunning in dealing with their adult leaders and will create interpersonal barriers and display ongoing resistance with such vigor that the patience of most leaders will be tested.

❖ DEFINING MEMBERSHIP

The first step in working with young people in a group is to define the criteria for membership. These criteria depend upon the goals for the group, as well as the needs of prospective group members. Some professionals who work with young people in treatment centers have been called upon to lead groups for whom the cause for treatment has taken precedence. Leaders of these groups require specialized training and expertise. Assuming that the group is composed of a "normal" population, the group leader's goals might include young people's ability to improve their interpersonal skills and develop self-management strategies, problem-solving techniques, and active coping skills.

In the scope of this book, criteria for group membership are directed toward individuals who can, with the help of the group, attain those goals. In this type of group, potential members whose behavior is so bizarre that other group members will be frightened or whose behavior is beyond the mores of acceptance for group members should be excluded. These individuals are not desirable group members. Nor are young people who are character-disordered. Other unsuitable candidates include withdrawn or passive individuals and those who are so troubled that they spill their anxieties at an uncontrollable pace. Certain combinations of group members also may cause problems. For the groups we are discussing here, avoiding potential conflicts as much as possible is best. Like adults, young people with disruptive personalities place severe limits upon the group and render the group less effective.

Finally, a group should not be put together to benefit one person. Benefits derived in group work are for the group as a whole. If the group bogs down and members drop out, inadequate choice in membership is most often the cause. The choice of a group member, according to Corey and Corey (1987), should be based on two questions: Is the group suitable for the individual? Is the individual suitable for the group?

❖ GRADE LEVEL

When forming a group in the school setting, should grade level be a consideration? No hard-and-fast rule can be offered to answer this question. Nor is a significant body of research available to suggest that young people function more productively with peers of the same grade level. Yet, as a general practice, forming groups according to grade level has been found to be best. Not only are developmental issues a consideration, but students' social events and behavioral expectations also vary as they move from grade to grade. Students are involved in grade-level social events such as back-to-school nights, school carnivals, homecoming activities, and proms. The school is the social system in which group members function, and young people respond to these differences by grade level.

❖ GENDER, GROUP SIZE, AND DURATION OF MEETINGS

Young people in grades 6 through 8 usually work better in single-sex groups. During this time boys and girls are maturing so rapidly that their hormonal development encroaches upon their behavior within the group setting. Girls are developing faster than boys. Middle-school boys are in a stage of "love 'em and hate 'em." Girls, who usually are more sophisticated at this age, talk about boys' "cruel behavior." The boys are unpredictable in their behavior and their loyalty to the opposite sex. The developmental stages of boys and girls can have a turbulent effect on the group. With older adolescents, however, mixed-sex groups generally are preferred.

The age level of participants influences the number of group members and the duration of meetings. Young children, immature adolescents, and those with special needs tend to have a short attention span. In addition, they may be unable to give much notice to the concerns of others in the group, because of their developmental level.

The usual size of an adolescent group is seven or eight, which allows for dropouts. Once a group falls below five members, the dynamics change and the group becomes less productive. When working with very young children and young people with special needs, leaders should consider groups of three or four.

Time considerations for the youngest groups can range from 15- to 30-minute sessions, depending upon the children's maturity level. Meetings with this age group also are more frequent — two or three times a week. For adolescents, a typical class period meeting once a week, for a minimum of 12 weeks, is suggested.

Groups move more productively when they have a known beginning and a known end. Time limits should be set for the number of weeks the group is to meet and also for the length of the individual sessions. Above all, in adhering to time limits, consistency is important.

Once the group has been informed of the number of weeks it is scheduled to meet, the group's life should not be extended. If the need arises to extend the duration beyond that contracted, leaders might ask themselves: "Have I helped group members recognize that meeting individual goals is not strengthened by endless participation? Am I fostering dependency by continuing the group?"

SEATING ARRANGEMENT

Does the place where group members choose to sit have any significance? The answer is yes and no. Generally, the leader should avoid interpreting who sits where. Certain hypotheses can be drawn, though, and these can be tested as the group proceeds. More important, the leader should watch for neurotic pairings, such as adolescents who sit next to each other in every session and whisper, continually nudge each other, and snicker periodically.

If a neurotic pairing becomes a problem, the leader should intervene the next time the group meets. As the members enter the room, the leader should try to sit between the neurotic pair. Although the pair should be separated in a way that does not seem negative or controlling, separating problem members is essential.

GROUP COUNSELING WITH MIDDLE SCHOOL STUDENTS

Effectiveness of Here-and-Now Group Counseling

To conduct a study in the group counseling arena that meets the strict criteria for research is difficult. In a school, community agency, or private counseling setting, we often have little control over our clients, cannot find matched control groups, or lack constraints that will lead to reasonable interpretations of the findings. Many practitioners simply throw up their hands and depend on their professional judgment as to the success, failure, or changes needed in a group. Therefore, we term the following study "quasi-research."

Here-and-now counseling offers opportunities for collecting both soft and hard data. In any counseling or therapeutic group studied, there is a place for both hard and soft data. Soft data—how subjects feel about their experiences—often are collected at the last meeting of group members. This may be done through the use of a leader's subjective questionnaire, or simply by having subjects write how they feel about their just-completed experiences. Collecting soft data can yield valuable information, but it has a number of weaknesses. Most glaring is that members' emotions are at a high peak, resulting in highly subjective reporting.

Also, they might not want to hurt their leader's feelings. And because they could be easily identified by their written remarks, they might color their responses accordingly. As a result, leaders and the group experience tend to get more praise and higher marks than if the information had been completed in some other manner and at a later time. If data are collected at the end of a group experience, a follow-up survey would be helpful to see if the data hold up over time.

Hard data lend more objectivity to the process. We usually use a type of standard instrument and infer success or failure from the results. Although instruments are imperfect, they often lend valuable information to the researcher or leader. Hard and soft data both have limitations, but they usually provide some information that lends insight into what has or has not been accomplished.

Quasi-Research Field Study

In a middle school composed of grades 6 through 8, a number of here-and-now groups met each year from 1990 to 1998. Each year in the sixth grade, three groups of females were formed, plus one group of males who had volunteered for the project. Each group had eight students, and the groups met once a week for 9 weeks. All students who participated turned in signed parent-permission forms. Results are available for groups who started in the years 1990-1996 based on data gathered in 1991-1998. Sixth-graders in 1996 also were in the school in 1998 unless they had moved. This translated into 168 females and 56 males participating in here-and-now group work during the years noted. Of those, 16 girls and 7 boys moved during their years of involvement in the project, resulting in information for 152 girls and 49 boys.

Two counselors—one male and one female—were involved in leading the groups. Both had advanced degrees, with advanced supervised work in the group area. Both studied three videotapes (*Group Work: Leading in the Here and Now*, Carroll, 1986). In leading their groups, the counselors attempted to follow the concepts and procedures presented by the author while acknowledging that specific interventions at various times may be idiosyncratic and that Dr. Carroll's personality traits cannot be duplicated precisely, no matter how hard one may try. Nevertheless, her methods of leadership and intervention served as a guide to the leaders throughout their years of working with the here-and-now groups.

As part of an overall school evaluation program, all students in the school took the *Self-Esteem Inventory* (SEI) (Coopersmith, 1981) in October of each school year. Thus, the sixth-graders involved in the here-and-now group counseling took the SEI three times, once in each of the three grades. These served as pre-, post-, and post-post measures for purposes of this field study. In addition, the grade-point averages (GPAs) of all students were obtained from their records.

This study, however, is called "quasi-research" because so many variables could not be controlled. For example, a number of students received individual counseling over the same years, some worked as peer tutors in a school program, others received tutoring, some were from intact families, and others were in foster homes. Also, all were volunteers, which differentiates them from nonparticipants in unknown ways.

Field Study Results

Despite all the noncontrollable variables in this field study, a number of interesting and important facts emerged. For the *Self-Esteem Inventory* (Coopersmith, 1981), the mean score for all the sixth-graders in the school (over the years) was slightly above 68. The sixth-graders in the here-and-now groups had a mean score of slightly lower than 66 for the year in which they became group members. The mean scores for the total group of students in the school remained about the same in their 7th and 8th grades. The mean score for students who had completed the here-and-now groups, however, rose by more than half a standard deviation—more than 10 points from 6th to 7th grade. Their scores went up another 4 points in the 8th grade, while their total class mean score remained about the same. Scores were roughly the same for female and male students and for those who worked with either of the two leaders.

The grade-point averages (GPA) of the classes of sixth graders dropped as a total group each year they were in school. There were no significant differences between and among various classes. The mean GPA for sixth graders (on a 4.0 scale) was 2.93—2.78 for seventh graders and 2.72 for eighth graders—with no remarkable differences over the years. The GPA for group participants was 3.09 for females in the sixth grade, 3.18 in the seventh, and 3.29 in the eighth. For males, scores were 3.12, 3.17, and 3.26 for their 3 years of middle school. More important, the mean GPAs of males and females in the fifth grade, before they had entered middle school, were lower than the mean GPAs of their respective total classes. This makes the gains seem even more significant.

Follow-up

One and two years after participating in earlier groups, students in the seventh and eighth grades were asked to write about their experience in the here-and-now groups. They reported almost uniformly positive views about their experience. More than 90% reported gaining new friendships with other group members that had lasted over time, more than 85% reported an increased willingness to work hard on their studies, and more than 70% reported increased efforts to get along with siblings or parents. Participants said they wished the groups had continued for a longer period of time and that they should have more opportunities to be in other such groups in later grades. A number of students thanked their leaders for protecting them from students "who came on too strong in the group"

In conclusion, this study indicates that here-and-now group work can be an integral and supportive part of a total counseling program for adolescents. For those who believe in here-and-now group work, the data from this study may be used as part of presentations to administrators, teachers, parents, and other interested parties concerning how work time should be used. The results show that here-and-now work stands up well in comparison to and in conjunction with other forms of helping.

We should continue to strive to learn what works, what should be omitted in the future, and what should be revised.

7

❖ Co-leadership:
A Question of Choice

n debating the merits of co-leadership versus single leadership, we are left with the impressions of numerous authors and practitioners. Both points of view have supporters.

◆ ADVANTAGES OF CO-LEADERSHIP

Co-leading is the preview of experienced counselors, not two neophytes who feel insecure in their role and lack confidence in their interventions (Benjamin, 1978). For the experienced group leader, co-leading is a choice related to two important issues: (a) the philosophical and theoretical base from which the leader operates, and (b) the personnel available in the work setting.

In the past, psychoanalytically oriented group therapists spoke against co-leaders in group work because of the belief that co-leaders severely inhibit the effects of the transference relationship. Today, analytical group therapists are less united in their beliefs about the constraints of co-leading in respect to the issue of transference. Grotjahn, Kline, and Friedmann (1983) are among those who rely heavily on the transference process in groups and at the same time espouse the use of co-leaders. They declare that co-leaders are better able to monitor each other's transferences, as well as those of the group members. They see this as a major advantage in the process of group work.

Although most practitioners do not emphasize the issue of transference in group work, a number of authors (Bates, Johnson, & Blaker, 1982; Corey & Corey, 1992; Kottler, 1983; Shapiro, 1978; Yalom, 1995) support the co-leading model under certain conditions.

1. Constant monitoring of the group by two leaders is seen as a distinct advantage in that no member is lost in the process. One leader is able to monitor the group closely while the other can be working intensely with a single member. (Of course, working intensely with one member may not help the total group.) The more leaders, the more resources are available to the group (Kottler, 1983).

2. Group members benefit from the interaction skills the leaders model — as long as the co-leaders get along well with each other (Bates et al., 1982).

3. Working with a co-leader wards off leader burnout (Corey & Corey, 1992).

4. Co-leaders of the opposite sex are able to pattern typical male-female interactions, which allows for additional modeling. No significant research data show that the male-female model is superior to the single-sex model, although most authors cite the former as a preference. Yalom (1995) takes the stand that "you will be better off leading a group with someone compatible of the same sex than with a colleague of the opposite sex with whom you do not work well" (pp. 417–418).

5. Co-leadership allows two people the opportunity to share professionally what, under other circumstances, they might not. The opportunity for exchanges immediately after the sessions is particularly important for counselors who are relatively new to group work or are still group counselors-in-training. The novice or counselor-in-training can try out responses and leads and benefit from immediate discussion after the session. Whether the leaders are old pros or neophytes, each is able to support the other within the group process, and each will benefit from the debriefing after each session.

❖ DISADVANTAGES OF CO-LEADERSHIP

Counseling can be a lonely occupation. Just as in individual counseling, group leaders often feel isolated from others. Because of the demands of confidentiality and the safe haven that group work affords its members, the group leader cannot talk freely on the outside about group members. Even if the group counselor finds a colleague with whom to talk, finding someone whose clinical and theoretical underpinnings are compatible is difficult.

In individual counseling, one can recognize a therapist from a given theoretical system, such as cognitive behavioral, person-centered, rational/emotive, or reality therapy. Not so in group work, which has fewer "systems." Rarely can one find a "school" of individuals in a given geographical area with whom to consult. Finding a colleague with a similar theoretical frame of reference to share in the leadership is not too likely.

Despite the advantages of leading, and stated support for co-leading by major authors and practitioners in group work, the emphasis in university training programs is still on the single leadership model. Why?

1. Counselors must learn to work alone initially.
2. Training individuals in co-leadership is not cost-effective for most training institutions.
3. Learning to run groups takes time, and the university training program rarely has sufficient curriculum time to prepare co-leaders as intensively as individual leaders.

Shapiro (1978) asserted, "It is my firm belief that every group can be conducted best by more than one therapist" (p. 157). Although this statement may be supported, possible limitations should be pointed out.

1. Competitiveness among co-leaders is common, especially when they are new to the process. Leaders often compete

for member affection (like parents vying for the affection of a child). Or competition may develop when one leader, challenged by the group, receives little or no support from the co-leader. In both instances, the competitive behavior destroys group effectiveness. Selecting a co-counselor can be risky in itself. Yalom (1995) cautioned apprentices to "avoid destructive competition as well as obsequious nonassertiveness" (p. 417).

2. Most problems in groups run by co-leaders come as a result of unproductive relationships with each other. The matching of pairs can be as significant as the participant in a piano duet in concert or the players on a tennis doubles team. Each partner should supplement the other with a complementary style and technique. Intuitively and theoretically, co-leaders must be in sync with each other with respect to clinical interpretations, pacing, and response mode. Having similar personalities is not a requirement but, rather, a productive and creative relationship is required. This is a difficult criterion to attain.

   Examples of quality matches are Rogers and Hart, and George and Ira Gershwin. But, like Lucy and Desi, Martin and Lewis, Lennon and McCartney, a dual relationship may come to a point when it should cease. Co-leaders who do not work well together should not be together.

3. Attaining a balance between leaders constitutes another potential problem area. When a less experienced counselor joins a more experienced one as co-leader, the relationship is never equal. The more experienced counselor will see the need for intervention in the group before the less experienced one does. The experienced counselor will have to exercise restraint while the other gains confidence and steps up his or her reaction time to the dynamics in the group.

4. Co-leadership is not cost-effective. Can the institution, agency, or private practice afford two professionals to work with a small group? Finances become a significant issue when clients have to be treated in any of these settings.

❖ Epilogue

A GROUP ODYSSEY

Group experience can provide an electrifying insight into communication. The exchange of emotions and feelings can become a catalyst for thinking and learning. The group experience has no relationship to the monastic concept of contemplation or to the process of a group in retreat. From our perspective the experience truly belongs to the here and now, and the process is actually one of probing the here and now.

The outcomes of long-term participation in the group process are as yet unknown. The group under discussion here has met once a year for a sustained 3-day weekend over 16 years. The factors of age and life experience are most significant: professional growth and involvement, marriage or no marriage, divorce, remarriage, children, life, death, aging parents, retirement, changes in lifestyles, one's own age—all become interacting issues. As Virginia Wolf has written, "Time lets fall its drop." The group process perhaps exposing our very existence and selfhood continued over such a length of time has reflected these "drops."

An odyssey is a long wandering, a series of adventures and experiences that stimulate reflection, redirection, and possibly the clarification of one's goals, even oneself. This chapter is about a *Group Odyssey.* What follows is a description of the learning experience of this long-term ongoing group. In earlier chapters we have suggested interventions such as establishing rules (Chapter 3), how-to's (Chapter 4), what to avoid and how to circumvent certain roadblocks (Chapter 5). Sometimes our techniques create a detachment in the leader that can minimize his or her appreciation and understanding of another person. It may become mechanical: "This is what I do when." On the other hand, becoming too drawn to individual interactions can bias and possibly distort the leader's perspective. The counselor seeks the perfect balance.

We know from the volumes of research that change is not causal, and few agree as to the factors that create change. Working in the present without forcing group members to confront their deepest emotions as well as their personal past has preoccupied our thinking for several decades. The phenomenon of interpersonal exchange is a force that engages the psyche (the mental structure of the person), creating avenues for personal insight. The leader pursues the possibilities of these insights.

Looking back on the past years, we realize how few philosophical changes we have made. Instead, our convictions have deepened. What we seek is a therapeutic system that is congruent with how we view the human condition. This book—as you may have noted—is replete with the basic tenets of Irvin Yalom, whose work has yielded several decades of challenging, frustrating, baffling, rewarding, yet promising and productive outcomes.

❖ HISTORY OF THE GROUP

An invitation was extended to members of the New England Association for Specialists in Group Work to attend a 3-day workshop designed to refine group-leadership skills. Twenty-four people attended the workshop, which was held in a former convent school converted into a retreat house. The group of professionals who attended were, for the most part, in their initial full-time work experience. The group included a community college counselor, a director of student personnel in higher education, a professor of nursing education, 11 school counselors, a supervisor of pupil personnel services, three counselors in private practice , and two employed as counselors in social-service agencies. In addition, a counselor in a mental hospital, a part-time nurse, a school psychologist, and a full-time doctoral student participated. All participants held master's or other advanced degrees; ages ranged from 34 to 60 years.

Sixteen years later, two of the school counselors had become school principals, one an assistant principal, and another a counselor educator in higher education. One participant left public education to establish a private practice, another left higher education to become an organizational development specialist, and four retired. Over time, seven of the 24 participants have dropped out. The nucleus of the group has remained at 17.

◆ DEVELOPMENT

The paradigm for learning during the weekend was the fish-bowl technique, a popular training tool that many group leaders employ. Common practice is for those participating in the fish bowl to be observed by the remainder of the group. Periodically the group is stopped and the leader solicits comments from the outside group as to the specific interventions used. The leader describes how given interventions have led to group cohesiveness, trust and increased interaction among members.

A rule in the dialogue between observers and the leader is that there must be no comments about the behavior of group members or any attempt to diagnose individual behavior. A change in the paradigm for the weekend allowed for each person to participate both as a member and as an observer. Thus, the group experience was both didactic and experiential for all participants.

Three years into the training experience, the flavor of the group began to change. The outside group made fewer observations and asked fewer questions. The level of personal interactions among those in the fish bowl was deeper. The didactic portion of the workshop began to lessen. In that third year the workshop no longer was a leadership training experience but, rather, a weekend of personal exploration for the members. For the leader, the dilemma was how to handle this change. Group members began to experience the distress of others; they shared their own joys and anguish in this short 3-day timeframe. There was, however, no planned follow-up, no weekly meetings to respond to issues or unfinished business. In addition, the group had not been redefined. Was this a therapy group, a consulting group, a growth group?

In discussing this matter with a colleague (Trotzer, personal communication, June 25,1999), he said:

> The group you describe does not seem to qualify as therapy or counseling, a task/work group, or a social group since it meets rather infrequently but consistently over time. It seems to be more in the genre of a mentoring group and a growth group with longevity as a peculiarity.

He further noted:

> Perhaps a term that incorporates the aspects of growth and longevity would be apropos. . . . the group has a bridging quantity that reflects the life development of the persons and professionals in the group. It also transcends the typical group rubrics since it has become an ongoing group that had carved out a place in your life and the members' lives, making it a unique entity from both the professional side and the personal perspective.

Forthwith came the title *A Group Odyssey.*

What follows is a statement from one group member describing why the group was a constant draw. The comments expressed here likely are not isolated.

> Initially, curiosity and motivation to learn about group work from a highly skilled leader were primary factors in my participation. At the same time, I experienced some uncertainty and apprehension. I found myself very much concerned with how I would be received. Would I feel accepted? Would I feel safe? Would I feel a sense of trust in relation to both the leader and the group members?

> The sense of feeling safe and trustful of the leader came
> quickly. Feeling secure with others developed more slowly
> over time each year. I began to feel that certain excitement and,
> still, a little apprehension about being with the group again. I
> felt eager but tense. I wanted to see the others and to share.
> How would it be this time?

For group members, the beginning moments were risky. As leader, starting the group was also a challenge that continued year after year. An opening used commonly, "Who would like to begin," garnered no response from group members. In the past, this opening statement had worked well with short-term groups whose memories were in the near past. This group, however, came to the weekend with new life experiences and new agendas from those of the year before. Would the trust gained the previous year be lost over time? Only by beginning would one know. The waters had to be tried, but who would begin?

As leader, time was of the essence—only a weekend to be together! Another lead was tried: "What do you want to work on this evening?" No response. "Who has leftover business from last year?" Too early, too threatening. "What have you thought about coming here today?" No response.

At this stalemate, the temptation was to do the work of the group, as frightening images come to mind of the group in total resistance for 3 days. The enticement was to do an exercise or play a game; however, I was reminded of my own words (Carroll, Bates, and Johnson, 1997). "Opening every session with a structured exercise...is questionable " (p. 126), as well as, " The leader's insistence on using or completing an exercise may actually detract from spontaneous interaction" (p. 127). Yalom (1995) also has given warning, describing the consequences of hastening the process by exercises or other other forms of manipulation: "Exercises appear to plunge the members quickly into a great degree of expressivity . . . and do not develop a sense of autonomy and potency" (p. 445).

Regardless of how irksome it is for the leader, the burden of beginning must be with the group. This is the only alternative. In this stressful period of time, the simplest of openings do not come to mind. The following is an example of what worked: "Would each of you describe what your expectations are for yourself and for the group this weekend?" The key to this question was the word *each.* Every member contributed before interactions among the members began.

A unique aspect of the group experience was how the fish-bowl participants' emotions and interactions influenced the observers. Watching the group was like reading a book, like watching a play, like seeing a ballet. In this instance, the observer, experiencing another's sensations, feelings, or thoughts is prevented from actively participating in those feelings. Martin Buber described the experience as the "bold swinging . . . into the life of the other."

Despite this, the "rules" do not allow specific discussion of subject matter when the groups change. What outside members feel is simply internalized. Members are restrained from relating their agitation, anxiety, empathy—even the need to have an opinion or problem solved in relation to those whom they have observed. The leadership perspective here is to bring those who were formerly observers back to themselves. For example, a member now in the fish bowl might say.

> I was so angry at Dave. As I listened to him, I wish he could have the strength to have more discipline for himself.

This statement does nothing for the group process (Chapter 4). It keeps information outside of the group. A productive use of the statement would be for the leader to suggest, "Does the anger you feel for Dave have any relation to you? What are you saying about yourself?" Hopefully, the member will respond and more intimate interactions will begin. If there is denial, the leader breaks through the intellectualization and does not allow any more discussion by suggesting that the statement is really "outside" of the group.

Following are examples of group norms that are unwritten rules, including shared beliefs as to appropriate behavior for group membership. Although members were committed to the norms, reminders of the rules were necessary every year—for some more than others. Reminders include "Use the first person, speak directly to a group member, refrain from asking questions, speak to your present feelings, withhold the story telling." All are attempts to keep the group in the here and now.

To give the impression that the groups interacted intensively year after year would be an egregious error. There always was resistance of some sort. Kottler (1992) described Otani's (1989) basic categories of resistance, which were apparent in each of the working groups: "withholding communication through silence, restricting meaningful content, engaging in a manipulative style of responding, or violating the basic rules (p. 7). In addition, Yalom's (1985) claim to the emergence of hostility toward the leader was evident. Although it is not our purpose to discuss the factors, therapeutic or otherwise, that affected the long-term membership patterns, resistance existed in all its outrageous forms. Havens (1986) considers resistance as the potential for progress as clients seek homeostasis in their lives.

REFLECTIONS

Participants drove long distances from six different states. They were not friends who socialized with each other during the year. When the groups were formed each year, membership was assigned randomly. Participants did not complain about the constant flux in group membership. It was so much a part of the norm that one group member disclosed, "I held my breath when group assignments were given each year, hoping that I wouldn't be in a group with a certain person . . . the person with whom I had the most to learn. . . . Maybe I was scared to face the part of me that responded in a negative or unsettling way."

What brought people to the group weekend year after year? In describing clients who came to her for help, Dinnage (1989) said, "A few had a fairly well functioning life but wanted something better. Some knew exactly what they wanted, some just hoped for relief from misery, some found that they wanted different things than they had thought" (p. 13).

One of the participants reflected, "Although I don't see most of the members of the group—except for this weekend—once a year, there is a bond, a trust, which is difficult to explain to others. I never know what experiences will be revisited, what feelings will resurface, what pain will be triggered, but I am certain that I will leave with a feeling of being renewed and replenished, a stronger person for the experience."

Another said, "In the first few years, I was looking for tools, but it has gone far beyond that for me. . . . I have never felt so connected to such a large group of people who, ironically, I see only one weekend a year."

Group sessions lasted 2 hours each, after which the groups switched places. With respect to the change from observer to participant, one member said, "The two groups often interweave their issues, and membership in one does not exclude participation in the other, although it is less direct."

As stated, there was no discussion of the working group once the observers took on the working role. They do, however, feel deep emotions as the observers take them to the working group. A member said, "The range of emotions that I experienced would visually look like an EKG screen, spiking and settling into a rhythmical pattern, regaining a sense of balance."

Another reported, "Are there any emotions that I have not experienced? Listening to the other group has prompted frustration, anger, excitement, sadness, trepidation, happiness, regret, guilt, aloneness, shame, fear, satisfaction, contentment. . . . I have occasionally wished that I were in the 'other' group for one reason or another. . . . More often, I was overeager to participate directly in both!"

CONCLUSIONS

What expectations do the group members have for one another as they come together? Do feelings change about some more than others over the years? A member responding to this question said, "There was more faith and expectation for some, more than others. . . . The inability to confront, change, and challenge the self is frustrating for some. To hear a person be 'stuck' in one situation year after year and not seem to see it, or want to change it, and yet suffer from the position is hard." This comment mirrors Jill Kerr Conway's (1995) words, "One has to know the existence of one's rage or passion for change to transmit its energy to others" (p. 152).

At no time in this book do we make mention of group stages related to the group process, though some are wedded to group stages. Here, we take heart from Yalom (1995), who maintains, "There exists no empirical proof that stages in group therapy do or must exist. The evidence for developmental stages of therapy groups stems from uncontrolled, nonsystematic, clinical studies" (p. 303).

The group members described here did not go through stages. They were no more potent, no more intense, no more interactive in the 16th year than in the 4th year. During the years, however, the group often spent considerable time dealing with issues such as dominance, trust, and intimacy, then returned years later to the same topic from a totally unrelated viewpoint.

Did a certain perspective draw the group together? One of the participants has the answer: "There is something spiritual in intimate sharing, in experiencing and addressing common characteristics and yet accepting each ones uniqueness."Another stated "What I have learned from this experience has touched my soul, from what I know about myself, the way I feel about myself, my growth, my relations with people, and my response to living and being." And another said, " I feel l can look at myself as my own person. Sometimes controlling, angry, manipulative people can send my emotions stampeding (sounds like a wild horse avoiding the lasso's noose). Freedom always has been a big priority. My favorite song as a child was "Don't Fence Me In." The group has helped to implement that freedom both mentally and emotionally."

To this point we have not mentioned the stress, joy, and frustration of leadership. There is a temptation to preach about leadership skills, to give warnings about leadership dilemmas, to discuss the pain, the after-thoughts, the fears of counter-transference, the need to hold a hand, the need to be loved, or want to be ever-caring, wise, tender, and magical. Kottler (1992) suggests that leaders must have no fantasies of omnipotence. Instead, they must be able to move away, be rocklike, consistent, compassionate, yet firm.

The Group Odyssey has been an intellectual and spiritual wandering for leader and members alike. It has been a time when leader and members have been able, in Kottler's (1992) words, "to tolerate honest confrontation without running away" (p. 225). It is a shared journey of discovery. For some, "The traveling is sometimes so hopeful that arrival is shunned" (Dinnage, 1988, p. 12). Another group member contemplated, "That collective experience has led to a greater sense of personal spiritual awareness, increase in options, and appreciation of human sharing and connection."

Finally, regarding leaders, Kottler (1986), states that the force of our personalities demonstrates our effectiveness, as well as our willingness to be with the person in a caring and respectful way. He speaks of being genuine and the necessity to have selfless devotion to the group members as there is significant self-exploration during those 2-hour intervals. Life is an *Odyssey,* a wandering, a searching, a constant asking of the questions, "Who and what am I?" Bugental (1987) says, "We answer these questions with our lives, with how we identify ourselves, how we use our powers, how we relate to others, how we face all the possibilities of being human" (p. 5). The *Group Odyssey* continues.

❖ Appendix
Safeguarding Ethical Practice and Procedures for Reporting Unethical Behavior

One characteristic of any professional group is a body of knowledge, skills, and voluntary self-professed standards for ethical practice. A code of ethics consists of standards that the members of a profession have acknowledged formally and publicly to serve as the guidelines for professional conduct, discharge of duties, and resolution of moral dilemmas.

The Association for Specialists in Group Work (ASGW) recognizes the basic commitment of its members to the Ethical Standards of its parent organization, the American Counseling Association (ACA). The group counselor is expected to be a professional agent and to take the processes of ethical responsibility seriously. ASGW views "ethical processes" as integral to group work and group counselors as "ethical agents." By their very nature in being responsible and responsive to their group members, group counselors embrace a certain potential for ethical vulnerability. Group counselors must give considerable attention to the intent and context of their actions because counselors' attempts to influence human behavior through group work always have ethical implications.

The ethical standards of the American Counseling Association can be acquired from the chairperson of the ACA Ethics Committee by telephoning the ACA in Alexandria, Virginia: general: 800-347-6647: ethics chairperson: x274; or by contacting the ACA web site: www.counseling.org.

If a group counselor's behavior is suspected as being unethical, the following procedures are to be followed:

(a) Collect more information and investigate further to confirm the unethical practice as determined by the ACA Ethical Guidelines.

(b) Confront the individual with the apparent violation of ethical guidelines for the purposes of protecting the safety of any clients and to help the group counselor correct any inappropriate behaviors. If satisfactory resolution is not reached through this contact.

(c) A complaint should be made in writing, including the specific facts and dates of the alleged violation and all relevant supporting data. The complaint should be included in an envelope marked "CONFIDENTIAL" to ensure confidentiality for both the accusers(s) and the alleged violator(s), and forwarded to all of the following sources

   (1) the name and address of the chairperson of the state Counselor Licensure Board for the respective state, if in existence.

   (2) The Ethics Committee, c/o President, American Counseling Association, 5999 Stevenson Avenue, Alexandria, VA 22304.

   (3) The names and addresses of all private credentialing agencies in which the alleged violator maintains a credential or holds professional membership. These include the following:

   American School Counseling Association, 801 North Fairfax Street, Suite 310, Alexandria, VA, 22314. www.school counselor. org

   National Board for Certified Counselors (NBCC), 3 Terrace Way, Suite D, Greensboro, NC 27403-3660. www.nbcc.org

   American Mental Mental Health Counselors Association, 801 North Fairfax Street, Suite 304, Alexandria, VA 22314. eburnette@amhca.org

Commission on Rehabilitation Counselor Certification, 1835 Rohlwing Road, Suite E, Rolling Meadows, IL 60008. crcc1835@aol.com

American Association for Marriage and Family Therapy, 1717 K Street, NW, Suite 407, Washington, DC 20006. www. aamft.org

American Association of Pastoral Counselors, 9504-A Lee Highway, Fairfax, VA, 22031-2303.

American Psychological Association, 750 First Street, NE, Washington, DC 20002-4242. www.apa.org

American Group Psychotherapy Association, 25 East 21st Street, 6th floor, New York, NY 10010.

❖ Bibliography

Baker v. United States, 226 F. Supp. 129 (S. D. Iowa 1964).

Bates, M., Johnson, C. D. , & Blaker, K. E. (1982). *Group leadership: A manual for group counseling leaders* (2d ed.) Denver: Love.

Benjamin, A. (1978). *Behavior in small groups.* Boston: Houghton Mifflin.

Bugental, J. (1978). *Psychotherapy and process: The fundamentals of an existential-humanistic approach.* Reading, PA: Addison-Wesley.

Bugental, J. F. (1987). *The art of the psychotherapist.* New York: W.W. Norton.

Capuzzi, D., & Gross, D. R. (1998). *Introduction to group counseling.* Denver: Love Publishing.

Carroll, M., Bates, M. & Johnson, C. (1997). *Group leadership: Strategies for group counseling leaders* (3d edition). Denver: Love.

Carroll, M. R. (1985). *Group work: Leading in the here and now.* (Series of three videotapes). Alexandria, VA: Association for Counseling and Development.

Conway, J. K. (1995). *True north.* New York: Vintage.

Coopersmith, S. (1981). *The antecedents of self-esteem.* San Francisco: Freeman.

Corey, G. (1995). *Theory and practice of group counseling* (4th ed.). Pacific Grove, CA: Brooks/Cole.

Corey, G., & Corey, M. (1987). Groups: Process and practice (3d ed.). Monterey, CA: Brooks/Cole.

Corey, M. S., & Corey, G. (1992). *Groups: Process and practice* (4th ed.). Pacific Grove, CA: Brooks/Cole.

Corey, G., Corey, M., & Callanan, P. (1993). *Issues and ethics in the helping professions* (4th ed.). Pacific Grove, CA: Brooks/Cole.

Dinnage, R. (1989). *One to one experiences in psychotherapy.* London, England: Penguin.

Friedman, W. H. (1989). *Practical group therapy.* San Francisco: Jossey-Bass.

Gladding, S. T. (1991). *Group work: A counseling specialty.* New York: Macmillan.

Grotjahn, J., Kline, F. M., & Friedmann, C. (1983). *Handbook of group therapy.* New York: Van Nostrand Reinhold.

Havens. L. (1986). *Making contact: Uses of language in psychotherapy.* Cambridge. MA: Harvard University Press.

Hollis, J. W. (1997). *Counselor preparation: Programs, faculty, trends* (9th edition). Washington, DC: Taylor & Francis.

Hopkins, B. R. (1989, February 2). Counselors and the law. *Guidepost*, pp. 13-15.

Kottler, J. A. (1983). *Pragmatic group leadership.* Pacific Grove, CA: Brooks/Cole.

Kottler, J. A (1986). *On being a therapist..* San Francisco: Jossey-Bass.

Kottler, J. A. (1992). *Compassionate therapy: Working with difficult clients.* San Francisco: Jossey-Bass.

Kottler, J. A. (1994a). *Advanced group leadership.* Pacific Grove, CA: Brooks/Cole.

Kottler, J. A. (1994b). Working with difficult group members. *Journal for Specialists in Group Work. 19*, 3-10.

Ohlsen, M. M., Horne, A. M., & Lawe, C. F. (1988). *Group counseling* (3d ed.). New York: Holt, Rinehart, & Winston.

Otani, A. (1989). "Client Resistance in Counseling: Its Theoretical Rationale and Taxonomic Classification." *Journal of Counseling and Development, 67*, 458-461.

Robison, F. F., Morran, D. K., & Hulse-Killacky, D. (1989). Single-subject research designs for group counselors studying their own groups. *Journal for Specialists in Group Work, 14*, 93-97.

Rogers, C. (1970). *Carol Rogers on encounter groups.* Boston: Houghton Mifflin.

Rogers, C. (1980). *A way of being.* Boston: Houghton Mifflin.

Rose, S. & Edleson, J. L. (1987). *Working with adolescents in groups.* San Francisco: Jossey-Bass.

Shapiro, J. L. (1978). *Methods of group psychotherapy and encounter.* Itasca, IL: F. E. Peacock.

Shulman, L. (1979). *The skills of helping individuals and groups.* Itasca, IL: F. E. Peacock.

Spinal, P. (1984). Group resistance and leader intervention: An interactional analysis. *Small Group Behavior*, 15, 417-424.

Szasz, T. (1986). The case against suicide prevention. *American Psychologist, 41* (7), 806-812.

Trotzer, J. (1999). The counselor and the group: Integrating theory, training and practice (3d. ed). Philadelphia, Accelerated Development.

Weiner, M. (1984). *Techniques of group psychotherapy.* Washington, DC: American Psychiatric Press.

Wiggins, J. D., & Carroll, M. R. (1993). Back to the basics: Perceived and actual needs of group leaders. *Journal for Specialists in Group Work, 18*, 24-28.

Yalom, J. D. (1983). *Inpatient group psychotherapy.* New York: Basic Books.

Yalom, I. D. (1995). *Theory and practice of group psychotherapy* (4th ed.). New York: Basic Books.

Zimpfer, D. G., Waltman, D. E., Williamson, S. K., & Huhn, R. P. (1985). Professional standards in group counseling: Idealistic or realistic? *Journal for Specialists in Group Work, 10*, 134-143.

❖ Index